Hearts for Sale!

A Buyer's Guide to
Winning in Afghanistan

By Farzana Marie

Hearts for Sale! A Buyer's Guide to Winning in Afghanistan

Published by
Worldwide Writings, LLC

www.worldwidewritings.com

For Dr. Mohammad Saeed Niazi (1966-2013)

Unless a grain of wheat falls into the earth and dies,
it remains alone.
But if it dies, it bears much fruit.

Table of Contents

Word of Tribute

I am deeply grateful to many tutors on the subjects explored in this book. Among them are the Afghan colleagues I worked with during my deployment and previous service in Afghanistan—unsung heroes who consistently assume great personal risk to champion the values we share. The writings of authors Rufus Phillips, Terry Glavin, and Chris Alexander have been especially illuminating and inspiring.

This book would certainly be impossible without the wisdom and courage of Colonel Tim Kirk, U.S. Air Force, under whose visionary leadership our small team was able to see things differently, go boldly, listen deeply, and fight the war that is won not with bullets but with hearts. His contributions to this manuscript have likewise been invaluable. I am forever in his debt.

For commanding our unusual anti-corruption task force with a resolute yet broad-minded strength, giving us space to learn, listen, and utilize the scientific method, I thank Major General H.R. McMaster, U.S. Army, along with the rare officers who led from both the mind and the heart: Colonel G. Scott McConnell, U.S. Army, Colonel Rob Kearney, Canadian Army, and Colonel Tim Keppler, U.S. Army.

Lastly, I dedicate this effort to the memory of my friends, brothers and sisters of all nationalities who raised their hands to serve and paid the ultimate price in this conflict. May we pursue with dogged perseverance the cause for which they served and fought, in honor of their sacrifice and the ongoing sacrifices of their families.

Foreword

The mass murder attacks against our own nation on September 11, 2001 and subsequent attacks on other nations including the U.K., Spain, and India, demonstrate clearly the importance of denying transnational terrorist organizations access to the resources, freedom of movement, safe havens, and ideological space they need to plan, organize, and conduct these attacks. It is for this reason that the stakes in Afghanistan are high as we and our Afghan and international partners fight to deny Al-Qaeda and other transnational terrorist groups the ability to re-establish sanctuaries in Afghanistan. The stakes are highest for the Afghan people who have suffered during over three decades of conflict and now have an opportunity to secure a better future for their children. *Hearts for Sale* is a story of hope and possibility. It is also a call for continued support for the Afghan people and for more effective cross-cultural communication.

There is no one better qualified to write this story than Farzana Marie. I had the opportunity to serve with Farzana for nearly two years in a multinational task force that supported the Afghan government and people in confronting the complex and severe problems of corruption and organized crime. Farzana was exceptional even among our eclectic team of talented military and civilian officials. She possessed a rare blend of attributes that enabled her to go where no one else could. The Afghan people responded to her immediately wherever she went. Her empathy for the Afghan people and her listening skills invariably inspired positive action among courageous Afghans who were anxious to secure a better future for their children.

The ideas she presents here emerged from a synthesis of Afghan insight, academic learning, and practical experience. Farzana's engagements with Afghan civil society were critical as we endeavored to help Afghans secure their country from a range of criminalized adversaries, all of whom have thrived on the weakness of rule of law and are stakeholders in the weakness of critical state institutions. Her work in Afghanistan dramatically changed ISAF's organizational thinking and stands as a model for future counter-corruption and counterinsurgency operations.

The first time that Farzana briefed General John Allen, ISAF commander, on her civil society outreach program, the commander asked her to return to a slide filled with pictures of Farzana's team at work among the Afghan people. The slide showed the smiling faces of youths from around the country posing with Farzana as they worked together to achieve our objectives of supporting the development of good governance and rule of law. After pausing a moment to take in the sight, Gen Allen said, "This is exactly what I want to see. We need more of this." He went on to ask Farzana how long she had been in Afghanistan. She explained that she had served just over a year in country "this time." Curious about that detail, Gen Allen asked about her previous experience. Farzana explained that she had taken a year off from her studies at the U.S. Air Force Academy to come to Afghanistan as a civilian in 2003. General Allen asked what she did during that year. She explained that she had worked in a Kabul orphanage helping Afghan kids get an education. The commander then noted that her current service tour had gone longer than the average year, to which she replied that she had extended her tour to two years. Farzana made quite an impression that day, just as she did on all members of our task force and on the Afghan people.

Afghans would look at Farzana, an American, speaking fluent Dari the way someone might look at a family pet reading the newspaper aloud. Her presence was extraordinary and she was able to transfer disarming reactions into positive action. The ideas she presents are not theoretical; Farzana put them into action and proved their value to the conflict in Afghanistan and beyond.

Farzana's experience will help Americans understand better the stakes in Afghanistan as well as the prospects for success. Afghanistan has made extraordinary progress over the last decade in the areas of security, infrastructure development, individual rights, healthcare, and educational opportunities. The enemies of the Afghan state are increasingly criminalized and seen as the tools of hostile foreign intelligence organizations. Afghanistan's enemies are weak politically as they have little to offer beyond hatred and violence. The approaching Afghan presidential election in 2014 is already generating nascent multi-ethnic movements that call for further governmental reform, reject the political agenda of Taliban, and advocate enduring partnerships with Afghanistan's true international partners. In the pages that follow, Farzana clearly identifies important ways for us to continue our support for the Afghan people in this latest phase in their long struggle for peace and justice.

H. R. McMaster, PhD
Major General, U.S. Army

Introduction

It was Thanksgiving Day, 2010. Our team was geared up, traveling in two armored SUVs in the southern part of Kabul city, on the way to meet with a group of NGOs. Just as we were turning left into our location, a motorcycle tried to pass the front vehicle on the left side, zooming around it and clipping the front corner. An Afghan civilian man and his two children were on the motorcycle and went spilling into the street. It was a nightmare. Our team leader, an Air Force officer who spoke Dari, told the front vehicle crew to stay put and immediately exited the vehicle, followed closely by myself and our linguist, who also happened to be a medical doctor.

Colonel Kirk ran toward the crash, calling out to the man in Dari, "Are you ok?? Are your kids ok??" The man turned and glared, a look of rage and outright hatred on his face. Then it dawned on him that the figure running toward him in the standard array of body armor, helmet, and weaponry of an American soldier was speaking his language. He stood there, stunned. Then his expression transformed into incredulous joy. Joy. It was as if he had forgotten about the accident, about his kids sprawled on the pavement. *"Dari gap mezani??"* he said. "Are you speaking Dari???" "YES, I am speaking Dari," countered the concerned officer. *"Jur asti??*—Are you ok??"

About the time we got to the kids and started dusting them off, a crowd had begun to gather. Much to everyone's relief they were unharmed, and the man seemed keener to point out that our driver was stupid. We amiably concurred, engaging with him and his kids in Dari, to their continued shock. The man started asking us questions about our work and how it was that we came to speak

Dari. We asked his forgiveness for the unfortunate accident and if there was anything we could do. Amazingly, he declined, and instead thanked us for taking time to learn the language and show respect. We said our farewells and rallied inside the nearby compound, shaken but grateful at the positive outcome. Could simply speaking these basic but intelligible phrases in the local tongue, combined with a demonstration of genuine care really be that transformative, even in the most miserable circumstances?

That day showed that it could.

These notes and reflections are derived from two years of continuous deployment in Afghanistan, from March 2010 to March 2012, with three distinct assignments. However, my background in Afghanistan began when working there as a civilian in 2003 and 2004, with three years of prior experience living in Central Asia starting in 1996. My deployed duties took me on more than 350 missions "outside the wire," a rather strange expression referring to the real Afghanistan, off-post, where local Afghans live. The small team for which I served as operations officer during the last year and a quarter of my deployment experienced rare and extraordinary results, a few aspects of which are captured in the short anecdote above. This guide seeks to encapsulate the reasons for that success, which critically correlate to the "winning" principles in the ill-understood conflict in Afghanistan. It also explores the broader regional and strategic context without which it is impossible to understand Afghanistan and why victory through enduring partnership is so vital.

I write with urgency, realizing that in some ways Afghanistan has already been forgotten by the United States, even though many thousands of American men and women, along with our international and Afghan partners, continue to risk their lives today, as I write this. The stakes have never been higher, yet in many quarters, even in military units, one finds a sense of resignation accompanying announcements of withdrawal timelines while a myopic focus on troop numbers drives a highly uncertain environment in Afghanistan and the disintegration of U.S. national will for such an "endless, incomprehensible war." This too, on the backdrop of an active misinformation campaign by our enemies that has penetrated deep into the halls of our political leadership and national media, where one can hear enemy talking points unwittingly broadcast for free.

All this can only persist in the absence of clear understanding about <u>what is at stake</u> in the real war the United States, Afghanistan, and its allies are fighting, <u>where we stand</u> in relation to a clearly defined enemy, and <u>what is possible</u> given the resolve to move forward, never give up, and achieve a resounding victory that honors the desires of the Afghan people and the sacrifices made by many nations. This is a moment of critical opportunity which requires clarity on these subjects, the blocks of which can be built into a durable strategic framework that I contend has been missing in the past but is more achievable than ever right now, given recent events and the insight we now have at our fingertips.

"Winning" in Afghanistan does not represent some kind of twisted hegemonic pursuit on the part of the U.S. It is a moral responsibility to follow through on promises made, to make good on partnerships that have exacted a high price and demanded the highest risk for Afghans who have allied with the U.S. and NATO in order to recover and restore the nation they remember, the one they envision for the future. I contend that everything we need in order to win, is available to us—if we will only listen to the Afghan people and overcome the downfalls of our own bureaucracy. If the argument against continued involvement in Afghanistan is the high monetary cost, the solutions lie in simplicity and an emphasis on relationships rather than continuing patterns of wasteful over-spending. If the argument is the high cost in lives, we should not surrender and retreat, which makes a mockery of those sacrifices, but instead re-double our efforts to refine our strategy to simultaneously reduce the loss of life in military confrontations while maximizing psychological gains. This guide outlines highly specific recommendations toward clarified "winning" efforts.

Author with Afghan Hands and teammates Col Tim Kirk, US Air Force and Lt Col Andy Kreis, US Air Force

Part I: Strategic-Level Lessons

It may seem hard to believe that with a fine-tuned intelligence apparatus, dizzying access to innumerable sources through the Internet as well as human networks, and a relationship with Afghanistan dating back to the 1930s, decision-makers (both civilian and military) would not have the information they need to design a winning strategy. But there is a difference between intelligence and insight. In his 1972 debrief following the second of three tours in Vietnam, Major General John H. Cushman says the following about insight:

> Intellect alone does not guarantee insight. Soldierly virtues such as integrity, courage, loyalty, and steadfastness are valuable indeed, but they are often not accompanied by insight. Insight comes from a willing openness to a variety of stimuli, from intellectual curiosity, from observation and reflection, from continuous evaluation and testing, from conversations and discussions, from review of assumptions, from listening to the views of outsiders, and from the indispensable ingredient of humility. Self-doubt is essential equipment for a responsible officer in this environment; the man who believes he has the situation entirely figured out is a danger to himself and to his mission.[1]

Unfortunately many iterations and layers of strategic assessment and intelligence reports often fail to produce the insight needed, because the questions and metrics we tend to use generate colorful charts that rarely capture the heartbeat of the people. This shortcoming is all the more egregious, as author and scholar Seth Jones explains, in light of the fact that the

U.S. finds itself a victim of a strategy nearly identical to the one we used against the Soviets in Afghanistan: that is, the use of ideologically motivated proxy fighters trained and funded by outside forces.[2]

This guide presents some of the central findings and insights gleaned from our team's rigorous, flexible process of testing and evaluation, listening, and reflection facilitated by a very unique deployment. Three strategic questions drive the narrative of this report. Construction of a new framework may seem simplistic at first, but these questions and their answers mean everything to successful engagement in Afghanistan and future relationships in the region.

They are:

➢ What kind of conflict is this?

➢ Who is the enemy, what does he want, and what is his strategy?

➢ What does winning look like, and what kind of strategic, operational, and tactical approach will lead to victory?

What Kind of Conflict?

While deployed, I assisted with the development of a series of briefings entitled, "Strategic Glimpses," pieced together from critical insights we were hearing from the Afghan people and supported by the work of credible advisors, scholars, and authors. Colonel Tim Kirk introduced the subject of the question of the nature of this conflict with an incisive quote from Carl von Clausewitz's *On War*:

> The first, the supreme, the most far-reaching act of judgment that the statesman and commander have to make is to establish . . . the kind of war on which they are embarking.[3]

Most Americans, and most soldiers, understand that Afghanistan involves fighting "terrorism," a fight that we chose to take to "them," after "they" brought the conflict to our shores on September 11th, 2001. Some are able to define the conflict in Afghanistan as a "counterinsurgency" or COIN, perhaps adding that this represented a shift in strategy around 2009. Beyond that, though, the details are fuzzy. What, exactly, are we trying to achieve? How do we know when we're done? What does nation-building have to do with it? And what about this supposedly indigenous Taliban "insurgency" our troops are now facing—doesn't their existence and persistence mean the Afghan people don't want us there and we should just "go home"?

These questions represent some of the major gaps, flaws, and fallacies in conventional thinking about these subjects. Our team heard these questions over and over. In our pursuit of clarity, we stepped away from our computer screens with their endless flow of reports, emails, and tasks. Our leads and cues came from talking with Afghan citizens—at length and in the context of relationships and trust, far from government offices.

To the vast majority of Afghans we spoke with (whom we call "real" Afghans, those not steeped in corruption or under the sway of enemy influence), the things that seemed to puzzle us were quite clear. When America came to Afghanistan, we assisted in liberating the country from the colonial designs of Pakistan in the form of the tyrannical regime of the Taliban. Although some Afghans were initially beguiled by Taliban promises of order and peace after years of turmoil and civil war, it soon became clear that they were foreign invaders supported by Pakistan's Inter-Services Intelligence (ISI)—their CIA. Failing to recognize the scale of the effort required, or how deeply Pakistan was involved, America won a quick "victory" on Afghan soil with its superior technology and surgical, special operations-oriented approach.

Americans allowed Taliban remnants to flee across the border into "ungovernable" regions of Pakistan such as the Federally Administered Tribal Areas (FATA) where Pakistan claimed it was doing its best to round up the worst terrorist personalities for us. Post-conflict strategies of aid, reconstruction, and "nation-building" in Afghanistan were intended to fill the vacuum and build a strong nation that would be able to resist and quell these extremist elements should they ever attempt to re-convene. However, we misjudged the type of war we were in, and the fact that the environment was anything but "post-conflict."

Bigger than We Thought

This war is much bigger than we thought; it is a regional war fought with proxy belligerents and world-beguiling deception. Pakistan has been at various stages of war with India since 1947. Pakistan has also been at war with Afghanistan since the Soviet invasion (1979), and with the U.S. and the West since (at least) 2001, when we rooted out their fighting proxies (the Taliban) from Afghanistan. They returned to home base to regroup, gather and train new recruits, and plot their next move.[4] We have long talked about removing safe-havens, but the biggest safe-haven of all was deemed untouchable—because it was in the heart of our "ally," Pakistan.[5]

The recognition of Pakistan's real intentions and identity has been slowly seeping into the consciousness of the American people. Despite the ISI's best efforts, the exposure of more and more undeniable evidence, most significantly the discovery of Osama Bin Laden living in an ISI safe house mere meters away from Pakistan's National Military Academy, has led to a slightly increased level of public awareness on the role of Pakistan in the Afghan conflict. Still, few understand (or at least speak about) the broader implications of this revelation, while those on the ground continue to suffer direct and indirect consequences of this truth. One example came to light when 24 Pakistani soldiers were killed in a border skirmish toward the end of 2011, after which Pakistan responded by closing key supply routes and demanding an apology.[6] More on Pakistan's intentions, strategy, and the history of their involvement will be discussed in the next section, but the vital takeaway is that the conflict in Afghanistan cannot be understood outside its regional context, specifically the role of Pakistan.

9

Kinetic vs. Psychological

Next to underestimating the impact of regional actors, another major miscalculation is our continued focus on kinetic operations as the central and decisive military activity. Naturally, soldiers are trained and equipped largely for the kinetic (physical) battlefield. Military patterns of thought adhere to conventional military operational art—something for which the military apparatus is finely tuned. Pre-deployment checklists ensure we have all our issued gear, uniforms, and weapons—and know how to use them. Trainers certify we are well-versed in convoy operations, IED (improvised explosive device) identification, and scenarios such as Humvee rollovers: yelling *"rollover, rollover, rollover"* as you tilt past 45 degrees then crawling out of an upside-down simulator in full gear. But never did our training address the nature of *this* fight, the psychological battle-space we were about to enter.

We have convinced ourselves, perhaps, that those "nontraditional" activities not involving conventional military weapons are taken care of by the Provincial Reconstruction Teams (PRTs), advisors and trainers, Afghan Hands, Female Engagement Teams (FETs), and offices in charge of Information Operations (IO) and psychological operations (PSYOPS), whose job it is to field programs designed to inform, engage with, or influence "target" populations.

With no offense intended whatsoever to any of the functions just named (which are, in fact, critical), it is not enough to designate to a few people the task of winning in the psychological space. The whole war is psychological. Our enemy knows that he must defeat us psychologically to get us to go home. His kinetic operations—attacks, IEDs, suicide bombs, and so forth—are designed primarily for their psychological effects, not for the physical damage they are able to inflict. I saw while deployed a vast number of our military members already defeated psychologically: doing a job, counting the days until they went home.

The enemy knows he cannot defeat us militarily, so he is working overtime trying to defeat us another way—from the neck up. We play straight into his hand when we focus on the kinetic, rather than the psychological realm. The deployed environment is rife with a constant flow of briefings about safety, security, casualty reports, intelligence reports on "significant actions," and threats. These are certainly relevant and have their place, but never once in two years did I hear an official briefing that said, "Now remember what the enemy wants to do. He knows he can't defeat you on the physical battlefield, so he will try defeat you in your mind. Get your psychological defenses up. Don't let him do it." (And perhaps most importantly: "here's how" to do just that.) It's clear that we have superior numbers, firepower, and technology. But how can we win if we ignore the heart of the struggle we are facing?

In a 2011 interview, a Taliban website administrator said this: "Wars today cannot be won without media. Media is directed to the heart rather than the body. The weapon is directed to the body. If the heart is defeated the battle is won and the body is defeated."[7]

The enemy's strategy focuses on our mental and emotional defeat, and simultaneously on winning in the space counterinsurgency manuals call the primary center of gravity: the hearts and minds of the people. That is where our focus must be, too. The important thing is that as long as we remain in Afghanistan, at the request of and in alliance with the Afghan people, we are winning. The enemy is unable to accomplish his objectives and we are accomplishing ours—halting the spread of violent extremist ideology that has declared itself our enemy and the enemy of a peaceful and free Afghanistan. A genuine grasp of the conflict and a winning strategy both depend on recognition of its psychological nature.

Kids at a Kabul Kindergarten

Adversary Vision and Strategy

Based on the foundation of a regional, psychological conflict, we can understand more about the enemy's motivations and methods. As discussed above, the clear-yet-deceptive enemy is Pakistan with proxy fighters including the Taliban and other extremist groups. Pakistan uses these organizations for different purposes at various times, depending on which proves most effective, but al-Qaeda, Lashkar-e Taiba, Hisb-e Islami, and others are each sponsored, created, or influenced by the ISI. It is important to note that this guide makes a distinction between the civilian government of Pakistan and the criminally captured military agency that is the prime mover for policy and has become an architect of global jihadist aims.

The civilian "government" of Pakistan is not ignorant of this state of affairs, as it often claims. It too has much to fear from the ISI, which leaves a great deal of space for negotiation and diplomacy with the U.S. and other partner/donor nations. The 180 million people of Pakistan are likewise victims of the violence and fascism of the global jihadist agenda. With those distinctions in mind, we refer to the shadowy de facto state of Pakistan as the agent that continues to pursue ends hostile to the U.S., its allies, and all freedom-loving people, including young schoolgirls who just want an education.

The next section describes the history of the conflict with a bird's eye view on why and how the war exists today. Readers should recognize that any generalization leaves out large elements of detail, and yet even summaries like this one can get complicated and messy. Those who are not fans of "Game of Thrones" style intrigue should skip this section.

A Brief History[8]

Pakistan is the only country in the world founded solely on religious ideology. Tehrik-e Pakistan (the Pakistan Movement) was the major force behind its partition from the newly independent India in 1947. Pakistan is threatened by its nuclear-armed neighbor, with whom deep-seated rivalry continues, long centered on the region of Kashmir, divided between Indian and Pakistani areas of control. Pakistan pursues a number of geostrategic objectives: parity with India, the subjugation of Afghanistan as a province of Pakistan, being some kind of "geostrategic mercenary of choice" for Saudi Arabia and China, and extracting as much wealth from the West as possible. For these ends, Pakistan exploits tools best thought of as its four "A's:" **A**llah (distorting Islam for political goals), the **A**rmy (including the ISI), **A**tomic weapons, and **A**merica.[9] Pakistan employs a blend of these tools depending on the objective, and has played these cards well in creating a continuing advantage against their neighbors. India's perceived existential threat is not necessarily the prime policy motivation for Pakistan, but the promotion of that perception combined with a nationalist desire for parity with India dictate Pakistan's every strategic move. Pakistan idealizes itself as a victim of India's "aggression," and that legitimizes cutthroat, murderous policies. Pakistan's leaders see themselves as the rightful inheritors of the Moghul empire and therefore, the Pak regime has become inherently expansionist and hegemonic.

Perhaps the most compelling interest Pakistan has in Afghanistan is the seemingly intractable issue of "Pashtunistan."[10] If movements for an independent Pashtunistan (and the closely related movement for Baluchistan) were successful, it would rip Pakistan apart

14

and squeeze it into a narrow corridor between the lost territories and India.[11] The roots of the current conflict and corresponding policies date back over a century. In 1893, the British Empire compelled the ruler of Afghanistan to sign a treaty that formed the modern-day border between Afghanistan and Pakistan (the latter once part of the British Indian empire). This border, also known as the "Durand Line" for the crafty British diplomat who arranged it, runs directly through Pashtun tribal areas, family lands, and even villages. While this border might look favorable to a 19th century British strategic cartographer beset with a mortal fear of Russian invasion during "The Great Game" for South Asia, it was never helpful to the local population or for governance. Afghanistan has tried to reconcile the issue almost since the day the treaty was signed, with millions of Pashtuns affected and significant real estate for a much larger Afghanistan at stake. Afghanistan was the only country to vote against Pakistan's membership in the United Nations—and Pashtunistan played a significant role in that dispute.[12]

In 1960, Afghanistan invaded Pakistan's tribal areas in an unsuccessful attempt to press the matter of Pashtunistan. Afghan leaders from tribal to national levels believed that a significant portion of Pakistani territory belonged to Afghanistan or an independent Pashtun nation. Afghan leaders therefore sought to incrementally pressure Pakistan into giving up control of certain Pashtun tribal areas rather than face another territorial conflict. Unfortunately for the Afghan Army, this strategy failed, and the Pakistani Army won a series of military skirmishes in a rout. A furious propaganda war followed, and Pakistan began a long shift from defense to offense. In 1963, Afghan prime minister Daoud, under pressure for the army's losses and the flagging economy that resulted from retaliatory border trade embargoes, resigned his position. With his resignation, the Pashtunistan issue faded from center stage, only to reemerge a decade later with Daoud's return as leader in the revolution that inaugurated decades of war.

Pashtunistan: shaded area with striped portion on Pakistani side, solid portion on Afghan side of the border

Source: ICOS http://www.icosgroup.net/multimedia/maps/ Used by permission

When Daoud overthrew the king and restored himself to power in Afghanistan, the issue of Pashtunistan once more became a source of Pakistan's ire. Zulfikar Ali Bhutto, a Pakistani politician who had similarly resurrected himself after being fired for foolish military adventures, came to power in Pakistan in 1971 just in time to see Bangladesh's ultimate revolt against Pakistan's rule. (At the time, Bangladesh was known as East Pakistan and only gained independence after India's intervention on its side.) In that secession, Pakistan lost half of its national population (and the associated tax revenue), a significant amount of territory, and regional prestige—its political leadership also suffered a debilitating shame. Bhutto became very sensitive to any issue threatening Pakistani territorial integrity, and felt he had no choice but to begin sponsoring Islamist insurgents in Afghanistan in a strategy for national survival. Bhutto's logic was a reflection of lessons from Bangladesh: nationalist ideologies were powerful forces that could be dealt with by replacing them with other compelling-yet-friendly ideologies. Islamic extremism provided an ideal replacement, and Pashtuns were a prime target as native Muslims who might be persuaded to seek eternal religious goals rather than overtly political ends.

Afghanistan was in the midst of its own ideological struggles. Daoud ousted the king in 1973 by courting communist ideologues and leveraging Soviet-trained military leaders opposed to the bourgeois status-quo. These same ideologues soon became impatient with Daoud's indifference to their communist agenda, and a second revolution followed in 1978.[13] However, the communists were deeply divided between two factions, the Khalq and Parcham movements, and years of intense rivalry between them bred harsh tactics and winner-takes-

17

all mindsets. Incessant political infighting sealed their leaders' fates and condemned Afghanistan to bitter conflict.

Soviet premier Brezhnev personally favored Afghanistan's leader, Nur Mohammad Taraki, trumpeted support for him publicly, and privately promised support against several Iranian attacks on the western Afghan city of Herat. However, Taraki was vexed by a political ally-from-hell, Hafizullah Amin, a fellow Khalqi leader who had orchestrated Rasputin-style intrigue among the communists and brought a reign of terror to the Afghan citizenry. Even the KGB was cautious about Amin's level of inhumanity—and it is rather telling when the KGB is critical of excessive treachery and brutality. Since Amin was educated as a progressive liberal at the University of Wisconsin, some Soviets speculated that he might be a CIA agent in disguise (he apparently was not). However, such smaller concerns were rendered insignificant in 1979 when Taraki and Amin reached an impasse that resulted in gunfire exchanges, the assassination of Taraki, and ultimate Soviet political outrage over Amin's audacity, disloyalty and unreliability. The Politburo quickly ordered the KGB to invade Afghanistan in order to dispatch the proud and overconfident Amin.[14] The decade-long debacle that followed set the stage for further decades of war.

Between the fall of Daoud and the Soviet withdrawal, the Pashtunistan issue was reduced to a whisper amid the shouts of martyrs, exiles, and refugees for relief from the conflict. The Soviet invasion escalated Islamic radicalization with a simultaneous infusion of an "infidel" invader and mountains of money from foreign donors (including the U.S.) The ISI capitalized on this opportunity and established formidable insurgency expertise over time, while the issue of Pashtunistan faded from the geopolitical scene.

Pakistan now seeks a return to something resembling the post-Soviet era. When the Soviets suffered psychological defeat and withdrew from Afghanistan, Pakistan asserted control in Afghanistan through proxies, ensuring that Pashtun nationalism remained irrelevant. The ISI continued their Mujahideen momentum against India with a focus on covert war in Kashmir. Terrorist training camps and refugee recruits in the border regions supplied their terror campaign against India after the Soviet defeat, and silently grew larger and more dangerous. While the world looked the other way, Pakistan's "dragon seeds" grew into monsters and went on the offense.[15]

When Mullah Omar launched his Taliban movement in Kandahar, ISI forces were present en masse to provide support. The ISI initially negotiated equipment and financial support for the Taliban to open inland roadways blocked by Mujahideen warlords, and later intervened directly in Afghanistan. As the Taliban advanced toward Herat, then toward Kabul, over 20,000 ISI officers and Pakistani soldiers directly participated in the takeover.[16] Money from Saudi groups poured in to support the Islamic movement, enabling ISI to profit and gain power so that they could ignore civilian Pakistani authorities and operate independently. The "dirty little secret" was that Afghanistan under the Taliban resembled a Pakistani semi-autonomous region much like the FATA. ISI leveraged these lawless regions in the fight against India. Meanwhile, the Afghan people suffered at the hands of the Taliban, especially women, minorities, artists, and the educated. Many others have recounted these sufferings, both former and current.[17]

Pakistani military and intelligence leaders believe that

some version of these events will happen again once the U.S. and NATO forces leave—after psychological defeat turns into material defeat. As the ISI sees it, the West is close to psychological defeat and the Soviet history is simply repeating itself with NATO.

Motivation for Proxy War on Afghanistan

The ISI is an organization that seeks to retain influence built up since 1979, culminating in the Taliban regime when Pakistan treated Afghanistan as a colonial province and successfully suppressed the Pashtunistan movement. Since Pakistan's creation as what many believed to be literally "God's country" and protector of all Islamic people in the region, the nation has struggled to meet its people's basic needs or find much success in several wars with India. Radical religious views over the years have gained influence simply because the lack of success was perceived as chastisement from heaven demanding more devout (i.e. extreme) means in statecraft and policy.

This led fringe religious leaders to expand their influence inside and outside of government in order to leverage all kinds of sympathetic sub-national groups, from media to militia. The ISI became a prized concentration area for this extremist capture because of the organization's capabilities (refined by U.S. training and resources in the war against the Soviets). An institutional battle for control rages to this day.

Other ideologues in this struggle publically make secular and nationalist arguments, and acknowledge that the path of religious extremism is one likely to blow back upon the established order in Pakistan. These nationalists feel deeply the disparity between India and Pakistan, but do so more out of nostalgia for the days of the Moghul emperors and the original Idea of Pakistan gone astray. Their thinking contains vestigial British imperial notions that reflect their heritage, training, and customs as a former royal colonial agency. One thing is clear in the end, as Nitin Pai summarizes, "The Pakistani establishment fears that a strong independent Afghanistan—like the one that existed up to the mid-1970s—will pursue an irredentist agenda, claiming the Pashtun areas of Pakistan."[18]

Yet Pakistan is an Islamic nation that prides itself in piety, whether in substance or appearance. Regardless of the ideological pretense, extremist elements tend to flare up in punctuated acts of murder, assassination, and political intimidation as the ISI guides and supports its clandestine organizations behind the mask of Islam. This has a very intimidating effect on more moderate political leaders in Pakistan, and draws public attention away from the Pashtunistan issue. A strategic head-fake on this scale requires planning, indoctrination, funding, and an extremely organized and hierarchical military intelligence organization.

ISI, then, has metastasized into just that—a unit at war with Pakistani politicians, with the freedom-loving people of Pakistan, with India, with Afghanistan, and with the U.S., characterized by narrow political goals and the willingness to use any means necessary to gain the slightest advantage. They play both ends against the middle very well, and have played the U.S. masterfully when it comes to Afghanistan. As Pakistan expert Bruce Reidel put it to President Obama in 2009, "Pakistan is double-dealing us, and has been double-dealing us for some time."[19] In part, Reidel refers to large amounts of U.S. aid money that, though earmarked for Pakistan's assistance in the war on terror, instead ended up in the hands of America's enemies. Consider the fact that the

United States provided a record $4.3 billion for Pakistan in 2010 and think of the implications.[20] It is probably not a coincidence that the Taliban's insurgency perpetuated such chaos that Human Rights Watch described 2011 as "the most violent year ever" in Afghanistan.[21]

Among Pakistan's multi-fold motivations is a desire for unfettered access to Central Asia for licit and illicit commerce, and the only road providing that access runs through Afghanistan. Its territorial integrity at stake, Pakistan also seeks colonialist-style "strategic depth" in Afghanistan and a highly capable force of radical Islamic terrorists who yield regional and global reach. To fully understand the extent of Pakistan's intelligence goals, one must consider why ISI agents protected Osama bin Laden and kept him safe for nine years. They certainly could have gained favor with the U.S. by simply handing him over or "finding" him on the Afghan side of the border. Instead, they chose to keep him safe for some future purpose. This is a perfect example of the dangers of a military institution slavishly devoted to the ideological premise of Pakistan, no matter the cost.

The ISI is quite displeased by India's growing influence in Afghanistan since 2001, as Pakistan fears encirclement in an insurgent proxy war that has reached stalemate on the Kashmir front. Pakistan also sees Afghanistan as a pawn in its emerging rivalry with Iran, whose ports compete as inland gateways to Central Asia and deprive Pakistan of financial resources needed to fund the ongoing fight against India.

Lastly, many in Pakistan are angry at the international attention and aid for Afghanistan that is often perceived as coming at Pakistan's expense and exposing its rear flank to expanded Indian influence. The ISI is motivated enough to leverage a significant portion of their resources toward killing NATO and U.S. troops in Afghanistan. The Taliban is not so much a force from the local population resisting foreign "occupation" as a well-trained and supplied ISI proxy sent to bleed coalition forces dry even as Pakistan publicly claims to be our ally in the war.

Ordinary Afghans clearly identify Pakistan as the enemy. It is important for Americans to realize that average, moderate Afghans consider the Taliban and other extremist groups like Haqqani neither real Afghans nor real Muslims. An anecdote illustrates this point well:

"Rayana" was a Pashtun widow and mother of several children who worked at ISAF. I saw her almost daily and we would often stop to talk. One day, after a particularly deadly suicide attack in the capital, we greeted each other with a weary, knowing look. She shook her head as her face filled with anger. I asked her opinion about the extremists behind the attack. "These men are not Muslims," she said. "They are not even human. How can they think that it pleases God to destroy other human beings, innocent women and children, even fellow Muslims? They make a fuss over someone burning a Qur'an, but what is more precious to God? A book or a human being, His creation?"

Summary: Adversary Vision and Strategy

Understanding that the Taliban and other extremist groups are pawns, our focus on the Pakistani ISI continues with an examination of their strategy and vision. The ISI is highly adept at deception and influence operations. While ISI portrays ISAF as imperialist occupying forces, the fact is that Pakistan seeks to achieve a colonialist-style agenda in Afghanistan to support its ongoing adventurism against India, particularly in the Kashmir region. The largely unrecognized truth is that ISAF has helped defend Afghanistan against Pakistan's imperialism by denying extremist proxies' freedom of action. The ISI also portrays the current situation as a stalemate; this is one of their key talking points.

ISI psychological operations aim to make the U.S. and its coalition partners:

- Stay scared of the Afghan people
- Separate from the people – not thinking, just acting
- Try no new things – forget the scientific method
- Stay on the psychological defensive – forget about psychological offensive
- Not fortify our minds or help our troops fortify theirs
- Focus on the conventional – forget COIN
- Do our time, draw a paycheck, get a medal, and go home[22]

This is exactly what our enemy seeks. We should not oblige him. As our task force commander General McMaster often said, tongue-in-cheek, "Shouldn't we at least try to win? I mean, we came all this way!" Saying this does not suggest that there isn't plenty of ignorance and well-deserved criticism for our side, but it is important to understand our enemy's intentions on the psychological battlefield and seek to counter his efforts. Even if we do everything else right through "soft power" and diplomatic efforts, if we ignore the enemy, we will still lose this war.

Pakistan's current strategic vision is to win the waiting game. Every negotiation, peace process, or settlement is an attempt to play us. They believe "The West has all the watches and we have all the time"—that it is only a matter of time until the U.S. succumbs to Pakistan's demands. A central objective for Pakistan is the withdrawal of ISAF forces from Afghanistan, and their agents are pursuing this goal by attacking U.S. and NATO will, wearing us out, keeping our minds off the main objective and distracted from the real threats—and the real facts. Know that when you hear "TROOPS OUT!" in the media or from a friend, you are hearing our enemy's talking points.

I argue here that the issue of Pakistan's double-dealing hypocrisy must be recognized and addressed as part of the strategic equation in Afghanistan. But this does not equate to advocacy for indefinitely sustaining high numbers of U.S./NATO combat troops in country or escalating military operations in Afghanistan. It is precisely the focus on this issue of numbers as strategy that has blinded us. The message that we send to both allies and enemies, on the other hand, is vital. Regardless of how sizeable a presence the U.S. retains and for what purpose (combat or training), the heart of the issue is whether we are perceived to have given up and abandoned the Afghan people. In a psychological war, communication is key to shaping people's perceptions, and the people's perceptions determine outcomes.

ISAF COMMANDER'S
COIN GUIDANCE
24 POINTS

1. Secure and serve the population
2. Live among the people
3. Help confront the culture of impunity
4. Help Afghans build accountability government
5. Pursue the enemy relentlessly
6. Fight hard and fight with discipline
7. Identify corrupt officials
8. Hold what we secure
9. Foster lasting relationships
10. Money is ammo; don't put it in the wrong hands
11. Be a good guest
12. Consult and build relationships, but not just with those who seek us out
13. Walk
14. Act as one team
15. Partner with ANSF
16. Promote local re-integration
17. Be first with the truth
18. Fight the information war aggressively
19. Manage expectations
20. Live our values
21. Maintain continuity thru transactions
22. Empower subordinates
23. Win the battle of wits
24. Exercise initiative

Picture of a wall-poster at a Forward Operating Base (FOB) in Eastern Afghanistan

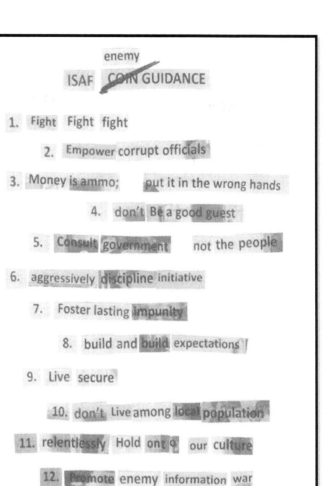

enemy

ISAF ~~COIN~~ GUIDANCE

1. Fight Fight fight

2. Empower corrupt officials

3. Money is ammo; put it in the wrong hands

4. don't Be a good guest

5. Consult government not the people

6. aggressively discipline initiative

7. Foster lasting impunity

8. build and build expectations

9. Live secure

10. don't Live among local population

11. relentlessly Hold onto our culture

12. Promote enemy information war

Created by the author entirely with words from ISAF Commander's COIN Guidance

Winning Vision and Strategy

U.S. ideas of what "winning" means in Afghanistan vary, and have changed over time. Even in the deployed environment, there was a broad spectrum of ideas about the topic, some better informed than others. Some have described the original post-9/11 mission as quite narrow: to pursue, punish, and uproot those responsible for the carnage on U.S. shores, specifically al-Qaeda and Osama Bin Laden. They say that mission-creep has led to the nation-building and development aspects of our involvement in Afghanistan, perceiving these as an "extra" humanitarian project not essential to killing, capturing, or otherwise militarily defeating our enemies.

Some even go so far as to say that such nation-building efforts are fruitless because Afghanistan cannot really be called a nation, and is basically ungovernable, tribal, and prone to perpetual war. Not only are these ideas inaccurate, they are racist. Yet one hears these kinds of comments with disturbing frequency.

After a major strategic review the White House stated in 2009 that the core goal of the U.S. was "to disrupt, dismantle, and defeat al Qaeda and its safe havens in Pakistan, and to prevent their return to Pakistan or Afghanistan."[23] In a 2009 testimony before congress, John Nagl described the end-state as "a sustainable system of governance that can effectively combat the insurgency, and in doing so prevent a reemergence of transnational terror safe havens."[24] It is generally accepted that in order to deny these safe havens, a certain level of governance and functional indigenous security forces are required. Education, health, and other critical services must reach communities in rural areas, which is where the majority of Afghans live.

While significant progress has been made in these areas in recent years, they are not quick-fix items. Many onlookers (generally those far from the conflict) fear that the Afghanistan "project" will go on into infinity unless it is given a clear end-DATE, rather than a clearly defined end-STATE, and the 2014 "deadline" appeals to that sentiment. On the ground, however, news of "2014" is cause for considerable despair. Announcing a U.S. date of departure is a dream come true for our enemies and feels like a death sentence (or at least exile, if they're lucky) to Afghans who have expressed moderate, pro-Western, or pro-democratic views. Many assume the Taliban's next bid for power (backed, as always, by Pakistan's ISI) will be in 2014 or shortly thereafter, barring a significant change in momentum.[25]

As one Afghan colleague once told us, "The Taliban have a clear patron [ISI]. They have a safe haven [in Pakistan]. And they have a clear vision of a post-ISAF Afghanistan. But what about the reform-minded Afghans who are on your side? They do not have a clear patron [everyone knows you are leaving]. They do not have a safe haven [everyone knows how hard it is to get visas or asylum, especially to America]. And they do not have a clear vision of a post-ISAF Afghanistan." A growing network of Afghan intellectuals, government leaders, media personalities, civil society activists, and young Afghans across the board is in fact dialoguing about a vision for the future of their country, to provide greater hope and social cohesion in an uncertain time. But this is admittedly tough to do in what feels like the prelude to a reprise of the abandon by Western partners, specifically the U.S. that many still remember from the early 1990s after the Soviet withdrawal.

A Vision of Our Own

A clear, shared vision for a post-ISAF Afghanistan is the crucial foundation on which to build future international engagement and partnership. Visionary thinking and action must replace harmful chatter about withdrawal, which smacks of defeat to both U.S. allies and enemies. Here are a few ideas on what a winning vision looks like for the U.S. and its Afghan and international partners:

> ➤ An Afghanistan not subjected to an extremist ISI or other foreign agenda, and invulnerable to exploitation as a lawless training ground and launching pad for future jihadist plots at home or across the globe (see White House "core goal" above).

> ➤ A long-term international partnership with Afghanistan as an independent developing leader in the heart of Asia (where the majority of the world's population lives). This requires governance reaching rural Afghan communities with provision of justice, security, and basic services, thus able to repel and subdue any lawless or extremist elements.

> ➤ Equivalent results to those achieved in South Korea, where the U.S., South Korea, and partner nations contained *and continue to contain* the totalitarian threat emanating from the North. Meanwhile, on the friendly side of the border, a nation heals, grows, and thrives, creating a stark contrast to the fruits of tyranny and oppression. (For a more detailed analysis of the relevance of the South Korea example, please see the afterword.)

Based on current policy, the ongoing combat aspect of Operation Enduring Freedom will continue until the end of 2014, when all combat troops are supposed to be withdrawn. Increasingly, the Afghan National Security Forces (ANSF) are assuming their functions, with great success and at a great cost.[26] Many Afghan units are still advised by coalition partner units and some number of international troops will likely remain in training and advisory roles beyond 2014, as they significantly shift the force structure. This transition does not have to be at all disastrous; in fact, it can be seen as a momentous opportunity. Fewer numbers and a shift away from the combat role may enable the U.S. to focus smaller, more specialized teams on effects that align with the Afghan vision and depend on Afghan leadership.

Winning in Afghanistan has never been about troops or dollar numbers. In fact, an excess of both has sometimes done damage. The genius is with the Afghan people, and long-term strategies for fruitful partnership with a stable Afghanistan on the road to healing involve being as close to the Afghan people as possible.

With that in mind, how we communicate about withdrawal or "security transition" has a profound impact. A psychologically attuned approach to complement decreasing combat operations is critical now, and must continue well beyond 2014 to assure victory. Otherwise, the tremendous investment that has been made, both in treasure and blood may be quickly squandered.

Based on observations of critical gaps, the renewed civil-military strategy needed now to achieve victory as described above requires a three-tiered psychological approach:

1. Agape: Win the people

2. Word as sword: Communication as our most powerful "weapon" in COIN

3. Resolve: Play the long game

Agape: Win the People

One of the four Greek words for love, agape, can be defined as a sacrificial kind of love: *undefeatable benevolence, unconquerable goodwill.* While military members often perform functions and roles that require severity and violence, a counterinsurgency context requires what could be thought of as the opposite approach, one of gentleness and devoted, sincere goodwill toward the people. COIN also requires the ability to identify and adjust to the situation's demands.

How effectively can well-trained U.S./NATO fighters make that transition, shifting from a situation demanding harshness to one requiring gentleness, respect, and even… love? Some do it quite well. Some not well at all. For this reason, those with natural affinities and capabilities in areas of cross-cultural communication, language acquisition, and informal diplomacy and negotiation should be identified and assigned to utilize and refine these skills for extended periods of time, even if it breaks with normal career progression and conventional deployment schedules. More on this in the section on headquarters staff.

A popular Bollywood movie, "Jodhaa Akbar," deftly illustrates the "hearts and minds" issue and offers us insight. In this historically based story, a brave young woman took courage and spoke boldly to a powerful

Mughal emperor who ruled India. She told the king, "You know how to wage war and conquer, but do not know how to rule... the truth is that you are far removed from reality. You do not know how to win hearts. To do that, you need to look into [the people's] minds, discover their little pleasures and sorrows, and win their trust. Be one with their heartbeat." Most of the Afghans we spoke with said similar things about Americans and ISAF.

There has been much ado about the now highly-cliché phrase "winning hearts and minds." Debates have rumbled on about how well or poorly this particular activity is going in Afghanistan, highlighting issues such as international and civil-military unity of effort, what is the military's rightful role in development and aid in counter-insurgency, and how any of the "softer" outreach, engagement, and assistance roles can possibly be performed by an "invading army"—a key enemy talking point that we would be wise to question. We should remember that they, too, are trying to win the people...largely by turning them against the international troops and the Afghan government.

When I think about this "hearts and minds" phrase, it occurs to me that when someone is trying to "win" the heart of another, it rarely has to do with carefully designed programs, expensive projects, or calculated messages. The process is dependent on the genuine feeling and motivation of the "wooing" party. The lack of authenticity in the suitor's gestures becomes apparent when he seems ultimately motivated by self-interest. This is what we observed with the Afghan people, who are exceedingly skilled readers of people. The intent is everything, and the intent always shows through.

A beloved and well-respected Afghan civil society leader,

Dr. Mohammad Saeed Niazi once told us, "The hearts of the people are for sale—but not for money." Genuine caring, respect, and service "buy" hearts; and those hearts freely offer the legitimacy governments embroiled in counterinsurgency so crave. Dr. Niazi's words suggest that neither the secret to earning the peoples' trust nor the sources of legitimacy among those people are found in money.

This concept is borne out in a study by Tufts University on the problematic relationship between aid and security. The study contends that "there is little empirical evidence that supports the assumption that reconstruction assistance is an effective tool to 'win hearts and minds,' and improve security or stabilization in counterinsurgency contexts."[27] While this may seem counter-intuitive, it coincides with what I observed in Afghanistan. Metrics revolving around financial inputs do NOT provide accurate measures of "goodwill outputs."

The Tufts research showed that first *listening* to communities about their needs was vital. "While the drivers of insecurity and conflict in Afghanistan are varied and complex, the root causes are often political in nature.... International stabilization projects tended to lay more emphasis on socio-economic rather than political drivers of conflict [focusing on]...issues such as unemployment, illiteracy, lack of social services, main sources of conflict, and in some cases fueled conflict by distributing resources that rival groups then fought over."[28]

Expensive reconstruction projects may even create negative COIN effects through allowing wastefulness and corruption, fueling rivalries, and undermining community leaders by failing to involve them (or failing to involve the right ones). The greatest factor determining whether financial resources invested made a positive difference was the community's perception about the project. Perceptions, in turn, had to do with the quantity and quality of government/donor interaction with the people most affected. In other words, the people's sense of ownership, along with their perceptions of respect and good intentions (or lack thereof) from the organization attempting to help them, determined the counterinsurgency value of the project.

This should be good news to taxpayers. The peoples' hearts are for sale, but *not* for money. Significant commitments in aid and reconstruction dollars, as well as the financial and personnel investment necessary to maintain and continue improving the Afghan National Security Forces, will certainly be needed in the years to come in order to solidify the gains we've made. However, an endless supply of dollars is NOT the most important ingredient in COIN; in fact, excessive spending often gets in the way.

My small anti-corruption outreach team discovered a surprising advantage: we had no money to spend. This freed us, in a way, to discover alternative, more effective paths to credibility and legitimacy among the people. Learning from our Afghan colleagues we began to tap into those sources, finding creative and non-standard means to do so and refining our operational mission over time.

One of the most significant things we found was that very often outcomes depended far more on mindset and intent than on specific actions. Actions do matter of course, but in Afghanistan many blunders will be forgiven when honest intentions are clear. As the Afghan proverb goes, *Niat-e saaf, manzel-e aasaan.* "Clear intentions, easy destination." We found many concrete ways of demonstrating those intentions, some of which are discussed further in the "Tactical Notes and Observations" section.

Word as Sword: Most Powerful COIN Weapon

Whenever a convoy leaves a secure base, its members go over checklists to make sure they have prepared themselves for any potential threats. They are armed and equipped with a variety of protective gear. But too often they are missing the one most important "weapon" that could save the day or get them out of a sticky situation—the ability to communicate.

One day a team from my unit went out in an armored vehicle. They were stopped by the city police, who were concerned that their vehicle did not have a license plate or proper identification. When the police began raising their voices, gathering around and blocking the vehicle from going any farther, the team inside began to panic. No one present spoke Dari or Pashto, so they did not want to open the doors, which offended the police even more. After a few minutes of this unpleasant stand-off, they called me. I respected that they did not want to open the doors; without the ability to communicate it could just get uglier from there. A Special Forces operator in the vehicle said on the phone he was ready to start shooting if the situation got any worse.

Finally, another Afghan Hand (a language and culture-trained officer) in the unit figured out to put my phone number up against the window, for the police officers to call. We first had them speak to the other Afghan Hand, a Colonel who also spoke Dari, and then the phone was passed to me. The officer on the other end was quite upset and explained to me the infractions and the rude behavior. Even though I didn't understand all the nuances of the rapid-fire explanation, I asked his forgiveness and told them the people in the vehicle had not intended to offend, that we would certainly take care of it.

After a lengthy conversation in which he made sure we understood that they did not like being disrespected in this way, the policeman on the other end of the phone said, "Alright. Khalas." *(The end.)* "Because of you and because you speak Dari, we will let them go." I expressed profuse thanks for his generosity, and we cordially said goodbye, breathing a sigh of relief as they let the vehicle through. In many everyday operations such as this one, communication turns out to be the most vital ingredient to achieve success or evade disaster: the most effective "weapon."

Despite this, we learned from hundred of conversations with Afghans, especially those outside the government, that perhaps the greatest grievance (next to civilian casualties) against ISAF was the failure to listen. Afghan colleagues lamented that U.S. and international forces often created programs and projects that were flawed, ineffective, or unsustainable, despite purporting to be well-intentioned. When ISAF people did talk with Afghans, they tended to do most of the talking themselves, coming into meetings with so many objectives and pre-determined solutions that a real conversation was rare. And the next "conversation" would often be with a different person, since the first had left and a new one had replaced him or her, in relentlessly dizzying march of faces, nametags, and business cards.

As my team began making an intentional effort to listen, we found the doors flung wide open for us. A chance meeting at a university cafeteria led to several more discussions, which turned into a student-led anti-corruption campaign. A soccer-field-encounter with the national Afghan marathon and cycling champions led to a citywide 5K "Race Against Corruption" and a network of athletes dedicated to transparency, integrity, and fair play. A meeting at Ariana TV turned into an invitation to participate as judges on a cooking show, which led to an invitation to host my own bakery hour, where I explained to regular Afghans across the country how to make the traditional breakfast tea-ring my family eats at Easter. During the show I also had the opportunity to speak about corruption, comparing it to a poison that would turn a seemingly beautiful pastry into the purveyor of a disease and death. These sorts of activities presented an approachable, "normal person" side of the American military most Afghans had never seen. We were real people. We smiled, we laughed, we baked bread. It was transformational, and Afghans agreed with us that a significant expansion of these kinds of simple yet genuine, effective communication efforts would be a game-changer in Afghanistan.

The reasons why communication is our most important weapon in COIN are found in classic counterinsurgency literature as well as evidenced in daily life in Afghanistan. In COIN, according to David Galula and others, a minority of the population is against you (and/or the legitimate government), another minority is for you, and the majority is on the fence, siding with whoever looks most likely to win or provides better chances of survival. That is why the population is called the "center of gravity," although I did not observe them to be treated as such in Afghanistan. Galula's first principle of counterinsurgent warfare names the population as the objective and the "real terrain" of the war, adding that,

38

"Destruction of the rebel forces and occupation of the geographic terrain led us nowhere as long as we did not control and get the support of the population."[29]

Winning in COIN is about convincing the majority that you (together with the legitimate government) are reliable, you are with them, and you provide a better vision and chance for survival in the future than the enemy does.[30] In Afghanistan effective communication of these ideas is not so much about clever billboards, public service announcements, or even the number of roads and schools built. In most cases it depends on whether people actually know you. Good deeds could easily be done for a variety of self-serving reasons and propaganda is produced by all sides. If they do not know you they might assume you built that road for your own transportation needs. Or to pacify some warlord. Or to transport drugs they heard you were flying out of your giant airbase back to America. How would they know? Truth and intention can only be discovered through genuine relationships. And those relationships, for the most part, are missing, frustrated by short tour lengths, high walls, and the highly insular policies of most military bases.

Other communication failures were shocking as well. The ISAF website, a place where educated Afghans might go to find out about the intentions and goals of America and the coalition, did not have a Dari or Pashto version. Whatsoever. Not even a few articles, perhaps the mission statement. Granted, a majority of Afghans are both rural and illiterate, but growing numbers are computer-savvy and curious. Our team brought this to the attention of the Communications division on multiple occasions (in January and February, 2012), even offering to help them create it, but nothing was done, and still nothing had been done as of July, 2013.

Many more suggestions for practically improving our communications and relationships with the Afghan community are outlined later in "Tactical Notes."

Resolve: Play the Long Game

In addition to agape-style interaction and effective communication, a winning approach in Afghanistan simply cannot be built on short-term strategies or short-term promises. In 2007, then-senator and presidential-hopeful Barack Obama referred to Afghanistan "the war that has to be won," calling the situation "precarious and urgent." He repeated that "losing is not an option," seeing it as the central front in our battle against terrorism.[31] When he became President, he renewed the commitment to Afghanistan by ordering more troops there and announcing a "new strategy" in March 2009. Since these remarks, however, the message of resolve has become more and more convoluted with the message of "leaving." In fact, that is all the Afghan people have really heard for the last few years, much to our enemy's delight.

As one Afghan civil society leader put it, "The international community has a big guitar and you have been playing the song, 'WE ARE LEAVING, WE ARE LEAVING, WE ARE LEAVING' that drowns out any other song." We have now communicated we are NOT staying until the job is done, but until 2014. Less prominent messages about an "enduring partnership" beyond 2014, or the number of troops remaining in the country after that time, are largely lost in the overwhelming hubbub about leaving.

In other words, how we TALK about the future and our commitment than the exact manner events play out in real life is even more important. Canadian journalist and author Terry Glavin described the connection this way:

> The way we in the West talk about Afghanistan has meant more to the course of events in that country than all the soldiers and guns and money we've sent there since September 11. What we say matters. It will continue to matter for some long while. It determines what Afghans hear from us, how much they allow themselves to hope for a peaceful and democratic future and how far they're prepared to come from the shadows, out into the light.[32]

Imagine the disastrous consequences of failed communication in terms of a counterinsurgency conflict environment. Your most important task is to win the loyalty of populations and communities who are "on the fence" and you just announced to the world that you are an unreliable ally who is leaving...regardless of what happens to the people. If they are hedging their bets based on survival probability post-2014, many may end up opting for the Taliban (read: the Pakistani army in Afghanistan), who are hovering on countless village outskirts applying intimidation and other social and physical pressures.

If it is "war weariness" and the loss of public support that has caused our nation and its leaders to back away from words like "victory," surely the answer is not to compound that leadership failure by fixating on troop numbers and timelines, while neglecting to communicate about core issues. The solution is not to back down but to educate the public about the persisting high stakes and the relevance of the effort there to our national interest, to recognize and honor the worthy sacrifices that have been made by so many Americans and their international partners (especially Canada and the U.K.), and to inspire them to victory. Yes, victory.

41

In the two years I spent as a military member in Afghanistan, I gathered far more inspiration to persevere and WIN from Afghans and our small task force than from the U.S. national or higher military leadership. If the Afghans who fight there at our side can show this kind of fiery resolve (when the human costs for them have been and continue to be immense) then perhaps it is time to step up our own determination, stop focusing on leaving, and start focusing on winning. This would make a monumental difference in the psychology of daily operations for the remaining troops, not to mention our effectiveness in communicating with Afghans and achieving our counter-insurgency goals.

Again, a lesson comes from "Jodhaa Akbar." When the emperor heard the woman's suggestion about winning hearts, he took two of his ministers on a walk outside the palace walls and through the local bazaar, dressed as locals and without bodyguards. One minister objected saying, "Your Majesty, why are you doing this? Roaming in the bazaar without guards is dangerous." The emperor replied, "Don't worry. No one will recognize me. I'm doing it since there's a difference between conquering and ruling. To win the hearts of people, one must look into their minds." In the movie, that simple gesture of walking around like a normal person directly resulted in the king's understanding of the people, and his elevation among the people as Jalaluddin "The Great" (now known in the West as Akbar the Great). Our team gained precious insight and unique rapport with the Afghan people because of the same principle. We were among a tiny handful at ISAF who left the walls and walked around like normal people, focused on listening. Such simple gestures went a long way toward "winning" their hearts and minds.

Author on Ariana TV's Bakery Show

Ten Propositions to Make this a Winning Effort

As a frame for discussing the more specific operational and tactical observations, I offer what I believe are the 10 most crucial changes the U.S. should make in our national understanding, policy, and operations with regard to Afghanistan. Each of these propositions captures both a principle or core idea and an accompanying recommendation. The *Strategic Centerfold* that follows is a condensed version of these propositions, included for easy reference.

1. We are winning a war we do not fully understand, and the fact that we are convinced that we are losing and should pull out is telling; our constant pursuit must be to question ourselves, seek insight, and listen in order to discover why and how this could be. Instead of mere "talking points," our outreach and communication strategies should *intentionally incorporate listening,* especially to Afghans outside the government of Afghanistan who have no way to escape the consequences of our decisions and actions.

2. We must publicly demonstrate an evolving understanding of the truth: Pakistan's proxy "insurgents" and "terrorists" are the enemy and must be publicly and consistently named as long as Pakistan continues to shelter, train, fund, and support those who seek to inflict harm on the U.S. and its allies, including the Afghan people. Diplomacy can follow from that hard truth.

3. The fight in Afghanistan is a psychological fight, and the greatest danger to us is defeat from the neck up. We must take measures to defend ourselves, our citizens, and our troops from damaging propaganda and psychological attacks of the enemy. Pre-deployment training as well as briefs in the field should incorporate this dimension of the battle and its implications for day-to-day operations.

4. The competition is on, and the prize is the Afghan population. We must do exactly what the enemy does NOT want us to do: grow close to the Afghan people and earn their trust. We have largely failed at this task so far, but it is in fact VERY DOABLE and will be relevant far beyond 2014. Those who excel at this (Afghan Hands and others) should be identified and empowered to engage and train others to engage as never before.

5. Language, culture, and good intentions are the most effective "weapons" we have in this counterinsurgency struggle. We must sharpen our focus on enabling and equipping all organizations with the practical tools to succeed in these areas, including dynamic on-the-ground training. Efforts along this line so far have been remarkably weak and poorly managed. This situation cannot continue if we are to see any success in Afghanistan.

6. Engaging with the Afghan government does not equal engaging with the Afghan people. While it is true that the government is made up of Afghans, most of these officials got their positions by other than democratic means and represent their own private interests and not the interests of the Afghan people. They are rarely, if ever, held accountable to the polity. Therefore, corruption and abuse has corroded the trust of the people in government, and we must engage the people directly at every institutional level, recognizing civil society's important role in creating pressure for reforming institutions, generating social change, and developing a positive vision for the future. While some might expect our diplomatic institutions to do this alone, such unitary engagement is not enough to provide military forces with the perspective of the people they so desperately need.

7. Authentic development takes time and cannot be rushed, surged, or expedited with cash. The amount of money spent is neither a measure of performance nor a measure of effect. Each potential aid expenditure should be examined in terms of its genuine value to the community and that community's ownership and involvement in its implementation. Strategic investments should be made in human capital and leadership development.

8. The DOD Afghan Hands program needs a reboot. The program must be re-fielded as a Joint Task Force and staffed with select members based on subjective suitability criteria who are committed to the effort for the duration of the war.

9. It is a lost opportunity that U.S. units and the Afghan Hands have few, if any, Afghan-American civil service partners. Both organizations would see exponential improvement if substantial numbers of Afghan partners were brought in as counterparts with Afghan Hands. Such an initiative would provide precisely the kind of expanded cultural awareness the military lacks today.

10. Communication with the Afghan people is a disaster. To begin, ISAF should at last add Dari and Pashto versions to its website. Rather than western-media-savvy officers leading the outreach effort from inside ISAF Headquarters and other bases, qualified communicators trusted by the Afghan people such should lead the effort from outside military compound walls.

It is decidedly not too late to make profound improvements that will influence the strategically crucial relationship between our nations for decades to come.

Author at International School of Kabul

STRATEGIC

CENTERFOLD

TEN PROPOSITIONS

Improvements to Make Afghanistan
a Winning Effort:

1. We are winning a war we do not fully understand; therefore we think we are losing and should pull out. To regain perspective and revive our engagement, we must stop talking and focus on listening to the Afghan people.

2. We must publicly demonstrate an evolving understanding of the truth: Pakistan's proxy "insurgents" and "terrorists" are the enemy and must be publicly and consistently named as such.

3. Afghanistan is a psychological battleground; the greatest danger is defeat from the neck up. We must take measures to defend ourselves, our citizens and troops from the enemy's damaging propaganda and psychological attacks.

4. We must do exactly what the enemy does NOT want us to do: grow close to the Afghan people and earn their trust. We have largely failed at this task so far, but it is in fact VERY DOABLE and will be relevant beyond 2014.

5. Language, culture, and good intentions are the most effective weapons we have in this counterinsurgency struggle.

STRATEGIC

CENTERFOLD
TEN PROPOSITIONS

Improvements to Make Afghanistan
a Winning Effort:

6. Engaging with the Afghan government does not equal engaging with the Afghan people.

7. Authentic development takes time and cannot be rushed, surged, or expedited with cash. The amount of money spent is neither a measure of performance nor a measure of effect.

8. The DOD Afghan Hands program needs a reboot. The program must be re-fielded as a Joint Task Force and staffed with members who are committed to the effort for the duration of the war.

9. We will see exponential improvement if substantial numbers of Afghan partners are brought in as organizationally co-equal partners.

10. Communication with the Afghan people is a disaster. Effective communicators trusted by Afghans should lead the effort from outside military compound walls.

It is Never Too Late to Win!

Part II: Operational Lessons

The American bureaucracy had become America's worst enemy. The Pentagon was too tribal.

~Rajiv Chandrasekaran, *Little America*

The section on "strategic lessons" described three aspects of a winning approach: agape, communication, and resolve. This section offers operational observations and additional concrete recommendations. These observations are derived from working on staff at both NATO Training Mission –Afghanistan (NTM-A), commanded by a three-star general, and Headquarters, ISAF, the four-star head-quarters for the entire coalition effort. The notes included here are ones that if addressed, I believe would make a substantial difference in designing and implementing a winning counterinsurgency strategy, which is connected to operational realities.

Background

I spent the first nine months of my deployment on the staff at NTM-A, commanded by Lieutenant General Caldwell, US Army, who was dual-hatted as the commander of the Combined Security Transition Command – Afghanistan (CSTC-A). My first assignment was on the Commander's Action Group (CAG), where I served as air planner for the commander. After six months, I was asked to extend my deployment to assist in starting up a new "Afghan Outreach" team. This was in fact a thrilling proposition, because I had just drafted the proposal and recommendation for such a team—after observing a severe disconnect between the military command and Afghan community.

NTM-A was the organization responsible for training the Afghan National Security Forces (ANSF), including the Afghan National Police (ANP) and Afghan National Army (ANA), as well as advising the government security ministries. The relationship between the Afghan force and the community they served was a critical one, since a key measure of success in building capable army and police forces depends on the peoples' perception of them. Civil society entities from media to intellectuals and think tanks could provide important feedback about these perceptions as well as credibly disseminate information on the development of these forces in preparation for Afghanistan to take charge of its own security. I could not think of any job in the military I wanted to do more than facilitate these relationships and insights. I thus became the operations officer for a new outreach outfit, a team of seven, with whom I planned and executed dozens of successful missions in the capital city of Kabul, connecting with key media outlets, universities, think tanks, and other non-governmental organizations who were exceedingly eager to speak and work with us.

Several months later, I was invited to work for Major (then Brigadier) General H.R. McMaster, commander of Combined, Joint, Inter-Agency Task Force (CJIATF) Shafafiyat, ISAF's anti-corruption outfit. There I worked for the "engagement and communications" team, and was charged with leading civil society outreach. Over the next year, the dire need for this kind of outreach throughout the country, its scarcity, and the reasons for that scarcity, became increasingly clear. During my 15 months serving with Shafafiyat (Transparency) I worked at ISAF headquarters, where I participated in the processes and functions of a four-star headquarters in charge of the entire Afghanistan mission, including multiple sub-commands, with personnel from 49 coalition nations on the staff. I gained respect for the monumentally complex and difficult task that this presented, but also witnessed many of the weaknesses that inhibited the successful accomplishment of that mission.

The following observations come from all three periods of my deployment.

"Tourism" and Short-Circuiting Insight

If "careerism" is an excessive focus on one's career, "tourism" in this context is an excessive focus on one's tour of duty. What I observed in Afghanistan was that almost no one was focused on actual overall mission success. Almost everyone was focused on one thing: getting home safely. This was innocently reinforced back home by those who naturally wished for their loved one's safe return but did not have a complete understanding of the high stakes of the conflict. For those who wait and pray, and especially for those who have lost a friend, a love, a family member in this conflict, it is all the more vital that we refuse to let this priceless investment be in vain.

For soldiers and leaders in highly hostile areas and living on small Forward Operating Bases (FOBs), a day-to-day "survive and make it home with your life, arms, legs, and buddies intact" mentality is understandable. Yet without the appropriate psychological fortification and context it can be very damaging. And this attitude unfortunately extends to the staff at headquarters and large fortified bases as well, which is anathema to the kind of innovative thought and action crucial to successful, unconventional warfare. Short-termism, tourism, and highly-risk-averse or conventional behaviors and policies short-circuit such thought and action.

These observations are not intended to downplay in any way the very real dangers faced by deployed troops. No one is arguing for rash or unthinking risks. However, when the refrain becomes "safety" instead of "victory," the mission begins to decay. If each person is individually focused on "getting through," doing a job, keeping his/her head down, not rocking the boat, getting a medal, and going home—who is left to figure out whether it's working? Or whether there might be a better way?

I saw the head-down behavior just described reinforced and rewarded at the bases where I worked and visited: in the capital, in the East, in the West, in the South. Everything is thought to run more smoothly that way. It is a short-term incentive structure, because everyone is there short-term. The short-termism also breeds a frenetic sprint-like pace that leaves no time for reflection, thereby short-circuiting the kind of thinking that might try to make "risky" changes. What changes are made, then, are often based on hasty, incomplete assessments motivated by the need to create material for evaluation bullets within the span of a deployment of six, nine or twelve months in duration. There is simply no time to employ the scientific method to test, assess, and improve programs and initiatives, because the turnover rate means we are constantly starting over.

By the time a new person (especially a staff officer) gets oriented to the predecessor's basic tasks, there remains about enough time to cobble together whatever "progress" is possible—and then endeavor to make the results look better than they actually are—before handing the reins over to one's replacement saying, "It may not be the best or fastest pony (or it may be missing an eye or a leg), but it's the one we've got, and we're riding it." Whether or not the job is complete (because it never really is), and regardless of whether it is done well, that person goes home, medal in tow.

Even very well-intended efforts are plagued and sub-optimized by the maelstrom of short-term thinking and requirements. Who, in this environment, could be invested in the long-term well-being of the mission? The whole system is designed to inhibit the sort of unconventional thought, action, and innovation that a successful counterinsurgency requires.[33]

Questioning or criticism threatens the system because there is no time to fix it, at least not before the performance report. I observed the fate of several others who spoke up when they discerned dangerous trends or errors in the actions or policies of the organization. They were pressured into silence, marginalized, penalized, ridiculed, investigated, and then fired and sent home with letters of reprimand. What are the chances for insight in such an environment?

One of the areas where I saw the damaging repercussions of these patterns most vividly was in the disconnect between the decision-makers and the Afghan people. Most of the ideas I have described in this book were deeply offensive to the establishment at the NATO Training Mission.

I was verbally reprimanded on multiple occasions for having the audacity to suggest we should seek to foster a deeper connection with the community in order to discover realities and blind spots in the training and performance of the ANSF that we could never discover by talking with politically motivated and often corrupt government agencies. The range of insults I and others who promoted similar ideas, especially the Afghan Hands, received regularly from high-ranking officers on the command staff are too crude and unprofessional to record in this book. Objections, prohibitions, and obstacles were issued to keep us as "contained" and as far away from the Afghan people as possible, contrary to the counterinsurgency guidance given by the Commander of ISAF.[34]

Whenever we spoke with Afghans, the damage done by this attitude was clear. Afghan media agencies who sought access to NTM-A leaders were disrespected and insulted. Regular Afghans were deeply concerned about police corruption and misbehavior that could be observed daily on street corners meters away from the fortressed walls of the camp, but which went unobserved and largely ignored by the organization in charge of their training, because there were quotas to fill, numbers to churn out. Improvements have been made in some of these areas with new leadership, but others persist simply because of the "tourism" epidemic that breeds insular, risk-averse thinking and behavior. One anecdote will sufficiently capture this set of observations. We call it "The Bread Incident."

The Bread Incident

It was November 27th, 2010. Our team had two missions that day and we were organized in a convoy of two armored SUVs. Like every other day, I carried in my uniform pocket a crumpled and well-loved copy of the "Tactical Driving Directive," signed by General David Petraeus on September 21st, 2010. Paragraph "f" read:

> Members of ISAF must work to build trust and develop positive relationships with Afghans while driving... Depending on the security situation, deliberately plan time to get out of the vehicles and talk to people as a part of mounted patrolling operations, taking every opportunity to interact face to face. When security allows, dismount vehicles and remove ballistic glasses and walk among the people. Buy something at the village bazaar; ask a shopkeeper how his business is going; ask pedestrians how ISAF can assist the people in the local area. Above all, always be respectful to the people.

We had some time between meetings, so I recommended to our mission commander that we do a "roadside engagement" in accordance with COMISAF's COIN guidance and "Tactical Driving Directive."[35] I was in the lead vehicle, from where we informed the other vehicle of the plan over radio. We discussed the best locations, and the team leader, Colonel Kirk, opted for a familiar location, the International School of Kabul, where we had previously visited to read to school kids and build relationships with the faculty.

The nearby "Brazil Pizza" shop and a bread shop where they make the traditional Afghan "naan" were right across the street from the International School of Kabul, where Afghan and American children as well as kids from many other nations go to school, and where we knew the security staff personally. It was about 30 yards from the police station for that area, as well as the neighborhood where I used to live as a 20-year-old civilian. Our previous trips to the area had given us a good idea of the security situation, and that area was clearly one of the lowest risk neighborhoods one could find in Kabul.

Our risk assessment complete, we pulled up to the location and a few of us, who spoke Dari, dismounted. One stood guard to watch for anything unusual, since we were "noticeable" with our body armor and helmets, and I went into a shop with our team's linguist. We ordered food, then re-connected with the team leader, to let the rest of the team know it would be about 15 minutes. We decided the dismount team would walk down the street to the other bread shop, with the vehicles following close. As we did this, the three of us greeted people in Dari as we passed, to warm and astonished responses from everyone we met. One lady recognized me from my earlier time in Kabul and embraced me (brave of her to do through all the equipment), nearly in tears on my Kevlar-plated shoulder.

We bought about ten round loaves of steaming hot naan and shared it with a few people standing nearby as well as the rest of the team in the vehicles. A public affairs troop also dismounted with us long enough to snap a few pictures. We ended the roadside engagement after walking back down the block to pick up our food, continuing to our next location and believing we had left a different impression of U.S. troops than local Afghans had before. In the words of one Afghan woman we encountered, "You're so different than the Russians were. You're so kind to us."

Keep in mind, no shots were fired, no one was injured, and the mission was a success—we filed a full report of the engagement upon our return to base.

A week later we were under investigation by command. The fear-steeped climate of the staff was aghast at our actions: we had "broken the seal," which meant we actually opened the heavy doors of our vehicles to engage with the population. This was considered radically risky behavior. It did not seem to matter that supervisors above our team had encouraged us to seek opportune moments to engage, incorporating careful risk assessment.

To us, the "bread incident" had been wildly successful based on COIN guidance. A U.S. Army Ranger captain on our team who had spent years in Iraq and Afghanistan was on the mission that day and assessed that we had meticulously mitigated all security risks. But to the leadership of NTM-A, the matter deserved lengthy investigation. That investigation of our team and two additional investigations that followed lasted a painful six months and consumed hundreds of pages, but failed to find that COMISAF's guidance had been violated in any way.

Fortunately in the end our team did not experience adverse disciplinary actions. Still, the unfortunate lesson was clear: with rewards such as a long investigation including hours of sworn testimony, is it any wonder that most leaders with the power to innovate within the boundaries COIN guidance are regulated into inaction? The fear of repercussions on one's career is a powerful motivator.

The Counterinsurgency Gap:
Engaging Government vs. Engaging People

Working at Headquarters ISAF, our team found a strange idea propagated among the staff: that civil outreach was "not our job" and that we should "leave it to the state department." This simplistic and widely-held view is not, in fact, viable, and has caused great damage to our counterinsurgency efforts and prospects of healthy relationships with the Afghan people. For this section I draw heavily from the document I helped draft during my last month at ISAF: an integrated Outreach Strategy that considers the importance of both "top-down" government engagement and "bottom up" civil engagement to enable ISAF's success. This strategy was approved by COMISAF in 2012 and has proceeded to implementation, but many challenges and obstacles remain.

Substantial research and consultation with hundreds of Afghan civil society groups shows that while ISAF engages extensively with government entities (sometimes to the point of over-saturation) and tribal elders further afield, civil society organizations and networks have been under-recognized by ISAF as prime-movers in stability operations. Thus, such groups are not adequately enfranchised or prepared to take on key stability requirements in counter-corruption, peace and reintegration, and reconciliation advocacy. ISAF has had little formal interaction with these groups where mutual understanding is fostered and public perception is formed. Our team's approach to outreach was based firmly on the idea that ISAF plays an appropriate role, in coordination with the international community and state department, to build governance, not just government. An expanded civil space in which Afghans are connected to one another crucially enables that process and facilitates the development of a broad-based vision for the future.

The Afghan people are seeking direct relationships with ISAF, to give their input and tackle issues that impact them every day, and the population deserves sufficient access to communicate their concerns, perspectives, and ideas directly to ISAF. As one student from Zabul put it, "Every Afghan can play a vital role to bring peace and stability to Afghanistan but nobody cares about us and our ideas." The success of ISAF's mission, likewise, depends upon this direct input, which has not been provided in the past by civilian partners. ISAF has tended to rely on surveys and atmospherics to find out "what Afghans think," neglecting to a large extent the irreplaceable personal interaction that not only provides insight, but simultaneously impacts those thoughts and perspectives through positive contact.

Currently many Afghans do not trust that ISAF has the long-term good and stability of Afghanistan in mind; the rest of our messages ring hollow without communicating real, positive intentions in word and deed. Lack of engagement in the civil space in Afghanistan leads to the perception that ISAF only talks to the corrupt governmental officials it has installed and continues to empower, especially in the national security arms, often to the people's detriment. This has contributed to the regenerative capacity of the insurgents and the manipulation of ISAF resources by criminal patronage networks. Not only the central government, but many district and provincial governments are ineffective and corrupt, blocking the initiatives of positive actors in government. Their empowerment risks continued alienation and radicalization of Afghan society, particularly in rural areas.

The Afghan people as a whole want to communicate directly with ISAF, largely seeing the coalition forces (and particularly U.S. forces) as crucial to holding back a civil war or another proxy takeover by Pakistan/ISI beginning post-2014. There is an enormous and under-utilized "friendly force" among Afghan civil society organizations and traditional networks, motivated and capable of doing everything necessary to generate community-based stability, meaningful opportunities for youth, and accountability mechanisms for government and the private sector in areas like human rights and corruption. They have a supportive role to play in each of ISAF's lines of effort, if given the opportunity. Civil society has its own dynamic that can reinforce stability and set conditions for security transition.

Through the continuing efforts of a very small number of people, awareness is growing in ISAF about this critical need and opportunity to engage the Afghan people at a decisive time. My hope is that many more military members will have the opportunity to make these kinds of meaningful connections, and know with confidence that they are part of the winning team—a team that is stronger than we have yet realized.

Good News

Though a small minority, military leaders could be found who did things differently, who cultivated their organizations to enable learning and creativity, allowing respectful dissent and careful experimentation with new ideas and approaches. Some even exhorted those willing to stay longer to do so, providing some continuity to the mission. I had the privilege to serve under several such leaders, which is why these notes exist. No organization is perfect, but an adaptable mindset that encouraged its members to think, to innovate, and to take bold steps bore results that spoke for themselves.[36]

Afghan Hands: Solution at Our Fingertips

During the course of my deployment I worked closely with members of the "Afghanistan Hands" program, or "AfPak Hands" as they are called when including the Pakistan Hands. The AfPak Hands or APH Program was established in 2009 to develop "a cadre of military and civilian personnel who speak the local language, are culturally attuned and focus on regional issues."[37] It was designated the #1 military priority by the Chairman of the Joint Chiefs of Staff, and APH personnel were to be placed "in key positions where they will engage directly with Afghan and Pakistani officials and the population."[38]

The program has fielded more than 700 military members, many of whom are now serving in Afghanistan-related jobs in the United States. While deployed, I became one of their number as an adopted or "honorary" Afghan Hand based on my language capability and local experience. The program responds to an absolute need, described throughout this document. Though the reasoning and vision for fielding the AfPak Hands is sound, obstacles to its effective implementation include the following:

1. Disconnect with the commands under which Afghan Hands served. The prime example was NTM-A, which maintained an antagonistic and hostile relationship with its Afghan Hands throughout my tour. Among Hands, it was known as a "prison" for those intent on fulfilling the mandate of the program, and most made every attempt not to get sent there, or to "escape" once assigned. Other units and organizations also earned similarly poor reputations, usually related to one or more leaders who did not understand the program or felt threatened by it.

2. A lack of imagination and technical/logistical support for unconventional and creative approaches to outreach, which were exactly what the Afghan Hands mission set called for. We procured, at our own expense, almost every piece of equipment we needed for our missions.

3. Recruitment. Many Afghan Hands were (and still are) non-volunteers for the program. This has had a very negative impact, because to be an effective Afghan Hand requires a high degree of personal motivation, inspiration, and talent. There are a variety of reasons for this situation. Many qualified potential recruits fear the impact on their career, which they are right to do, based on the experience of many currently serving Afghan Hands who feel it has negatively impacted their opportunities for advancement. Others simply do not see it as a competitive program, since the selection process is not overly demanding and so many were assigned to it against their wishes. Others, including myself, sought for years to be admitted to the program, yet were told that despite significant pre-existing experience and linguistic competence, it did not fit with our expected "career progression" and therefore would not be permitted.

4. Utilization. Over the course of around four years since the program's creation, Afghan Hands have been assigned by and large to pre-existing job billets that were designated as conducive to exposure to Afghans. Some have worked out better than others, and there has been an ongoing struggle to "rescue" Afghan Hands from billets that were entirely antithetical to the program's purpose. The other major issue was that the vast majority of these billets installed Afghan Hands in positions that interacted with the government, while only a tiny handful (most of them on our team in Shafafiyat) were assigned to interact directly with the Afghan people or civil society. The guidance for the program clearly stated that they were to do both, presumably in approximately equal measures. This imbalance reflected a harmful discrepancy in ISAF's outreach and engagement overall.

Other utilization issues include the Air Force's automatic disenrollment of some of the most experienced Hands from the program once they pinned on the rank of Colonel. Instead of sending them to Afghanistan-related leadership positions where they could use their insight to inform future decisions (like many of their joint colleagues), the Air Force sends them to jobs having nothing to do with the war effort, again using bureaucratic-thin "career progression" reasoning, despite their eagerness to continue their service in the Chairman's top-priority program. For example, Colonel Kirk was pulled from the program despite the results of his work and sent to a routine Air Force logistics staff job, despite the recognition by Afghans and clear-thinking Americans alike that he was a modern-day incarnation of Colonel Hillandale from the profoundly important novel, *The Ugly American,* which was based on real events and personalities from America's involvement in Southeast Asia.[39] Colonel Hillandale's character is likely based on

U.S. Air Force Major General Edward Lansdale, as described by Rufus Phillips in *Why Vietnam Matters: An Eyewitness Account of Lessons Not Learned*. Lansdale is one of the few Americans who parts with convention (along with excessive cocktail parties with other Americans) and engages effectively with local counterparts. *The Ugly American* addresses many similar issues to those described in this guide, which since 1958 unfortunately remain lessons-not-learned. Colonel Kirk, whose disposition and skills made him uniquely positioned to continue making a profound impact in Afghanistan, will presumably not work on that mission set for the remainder of his career.

The AfPak Hands program is a solution "in waiting" that could fill so many gaps and capture critical opportunities like the ones I've described here and those on which I will elaborate in the next section.

PART III: Tactical Lessons

On Language: A House with Many Windows

The rest of this guide focuses on observations and best practices for daily interaction with Afghans at the grassroots or "tactical" level. Naturally, these notes are most applicable to those endeavoring to build and improve relationships with Afghans, rather than those focused on hostile actions against enemy objectives. The general principles, however, are relevant for anyone who may encounter or work with Afghan people, especially in a deployed environment. If you do not fall into that category, there are plenty of good "war stories" you'll still want to read.

This section focuses on the practical angles to language and communication. The next section looks at lessons and best practices in the realm of culture, looking at both actions and attitudes that facilitate successful outreach.

Improving Our Fighting Position

It is impossible to recount the number of conversations I've had with Afghans about language. While deployed, the topic generally came up because they were shocked to find an ISAF member conversant in Dari or Pashto, and wanted to know how it happened. With approval, an Afghan would often recall the saying, "A person who speaks only one language is only one person, but speaking many languages you can be many people!" Or they make it more personal, saying, "Now we know that you respect us, because you have taken time to learn our language."

Another common metaphor is that of a house. With only one window (language), you can only see out in one direction. But with many windows, you multiply your awareness and understanding with a variety of angles and perspectives. You are able to see approaching dangers or opportunities, appreciate beauty and the changing of seasons. Windows also fill the house with light.

Approaching complex operations in a place like Afghanistan without linguistic and cultural expertise is like taking up a defensive fighting position in a building with no windows. You might feel safe for a little while, but without the ability to see what is going on in the surrounding area, the ability to anticipate threats or opportunities is lost, and you are actually extremely vulnerable. This recognition is what led the Chairman of the Joint Chiefs of Staff to launch the Afghan-Pakistan Hands program as his "#1 military priority," seeking to generate this linguistic as well as culture expertise, which are naturally intertwined.

In the military, lip service is given to the need for language capacity, while the vast gains that could be made through the effective utilization of language by everyone from general officers to soldiers on foot patrol are consistently forfeited. One does not need to be fluent to see the powerful effects of verbal communication in a place like Afghanistan. It has never ceased to amaze me how little language was required to produce profound bonding and respect. Often, merely a greeting and introductory phrases produce these goodwill shock waves; the first few moments of interaction could remarkably accelerate the speed of trust. That is why my notes begin with "greet like an Afghan."

Language Notes: Greet Like an Afghan

First impressions count. In Afghanistan, they count even more because greetings are a crucial way of showing respect. In a Dari language class I designed and helped teach at Camp Eggers, the first thing we did in every session was to spend the first five to ten minutes on greetings. Afghan greetings are very different from Western greetings, so it is not only a matter of learning the *words,* but learning the *way.* This is not only true of the physical gestures that accompany a greeting (easy to learn from observation), but also the kinds of words and expressions used, which are the focus here.

The first difference I saw between typical American and Afghan greetings was in the level of importance attached to greetings. When a new person enters a room in Afghanistan, he/she takes the time to greet everyone, as appropriate to context and gender. Not to do so is very disrespectful. Even passing strangers or vague acquaintances on the street or in the workplace without greeting them is very rude. For example, our team members always greeted the Afghan security contractors who guarded the gates of our camp. It was clear that hundreds of others walked by them every day without acknowledging them at all, much less greeting them in their native tongue. I believe that if one of them were offered a substantial bribe to help get an explosive into the base, a crucial factor that would make him think twice about it would be the loyalty built up by the courtesy and respect he was shown by the few who cared to learn and speak a simple greeting.

Another difference in greeting styles is the duration and quantity of words used. In English we might say, "Good morning, sir/ma'am" for a more formal setting or "hi/hello/what's up" for a more informal one. Afghans use a whole assortment of phrases in their greetings, many of them inquiries after health, family, and so forth. These phrases also include meaning-laden greetings like *Maanda na bosheyd* (Dari) / *Staremooshey* (Pashto), literally "May you not be tired," which pertain to particular contexts and have particular responses. This might seem a bit dizzying at first, but it is really a beautiful thing for a language learner because there is a rich pool of words and phrases here from which you can simply continue to add to your repertoire and practice constantly, mixing and matching as you grow in confidence.

The last difference I'll mention here is simultaneity. Typical greetings in English involve an initiator and a respondent, especially if the greeting continues into courtesies such as "How are you?" which is traditionally answered with something akin to "Fine thanks, and you?" Interruption here tends to be rather embarrassing and awkward. With Afghans, however, these rules don't apply. The better you know the person, the longer a greeting might go on, with both of you rapidly firing off greeting-phrases and how-are-you questions at the same time, not waiting for the other to respond but rather communicating your intense interest in that person's well-being via the "courtesy competition" that may go on whilst hugging, kissing, and/or shaking hands.

The name and motto for our Camp Eggers language course was "Qatra Qatra," from the Afghan Proverb, *Qatra Qatra darya mesha,* meaning "Drop by drop a river is made." Even though this is meant to encourage language learners that what feels like slow or small progress is significant, I also think of this idea in terms of the potential impact if every airman, soldier and sailor learned even just a little bit—say, how to greet like an Afghan. The overall effect would be extraordinary.

An informal Afghan greeting may go something like this:
Person 1: *Salaamaleykum! Chetor asti? Khoob asti? Familet khub ast?* (Peace to you! How are you? Are you good? Is your family good?)
Person 2 (overlapping): *Wa'aleykum-asalaam! Janet jur ast? Khona khairyat ast?* (Peace to you too! Is your body healthy? Everything good at home?)

There are many variations. If you are encountering someone who is working, you might say, *Maanda na bosheyn* (may you not be tired). They would respond, *Zenda bosheyn* (may you be alive), and then you would carry on from there. This is also a good greeting for someone who has come a long way to see you or is returning from a trip. It is also appropriate for someone with heavy responsibilities. *Maanda na bosheyn, wazir sahib* would be an acceptable greeting for a minister, since you might not necessarily go into the full "courtesy competition" with someone of that position unless you knew him/her well.

Time invested in learning titles and greetings is well-spent and sets the tone of an entire meeting or interaction, even if the rest of the encounter relies upon a linguist. Often, when you greet in this way, other tensions are diffused because it introduces a positive topic of interest right off the bat. The response is likely to be something like, "You are learning Dari/Pashto! This is good! Where did you learn? Who is teaching you?"

Here is a brief excerpt is from the article, "If You Look Carefully, You Can See It In Their Faces," written by Colonel Tim Kirk about language and greetings while deployed as an Afghan Hand. It was originally published on NTM-A's blog.

In America, like many other Western cultures, the significance of greeting varies greatly from place to place. Some folks say "Howdy, pardner!" while others say "Wassup, bro?" and the spectrum of responses varies even more so. Often times in our culture a greeting is superficial, insincere or even callous. Think about it the next time someone asks you "how are you doing?" As Americans, do we interpret this statement as true concern for our well being, or do we assume it away as politeness and reply with "I'm fine, and you?" in equal insincerity? It is important not to assume the same is true for our Afghan hosts. Their greetings are commonly far more sincere, interpreted as a sign of hospitality and goodwill. In fact to me, Afghans seem to consider the first few moments in greeting each other as a brief competition over who is most generous, most considerate and most gracious. When I first began studying the Dari language, I was impressed and intimidated by the initial 30 seconds of the greeting process... [a process which] sets the tone for the remainder of the conversation as well as the ongoing relationship.

I, too, have been consistently impressed with the overwhelming importance of the first few moments of interaction in the Afghan context, the urgency of communicating goodwill and concern for the others' well-being as the pre-cursor to any other meaningful conversation. Learning to greet the Afghan way may feel like learning unfamiliar dance-steps at first, but courageous learners will find a daily throng of willing and graceful practice-partners. In my experience, both the novice foreigner and the Afghan master leave the encounter with a twinkle in their eye.

Language Notes: No (Long) Vocab Lists Allowed

In addition to greetings, demonstrated language-learning intent is another tone-setter. Greeting and using a few phrases of local language in a counterinsurgency context can make an enormous impact, as demonstrated by our introductory story. Perhaps the most important aspect to successfully acquiring and utilizing another language is *deciding from the beginning to actually learn as much as you can.* Demonstrated commitment and strategies for active and practical language-acquisition provide a gateway to successful learning *and* effective engagement.

Some are intimidated by language-learning because it feels like drinking an ocean with a spoon and it seems unlikely that one could learn enough to make a difference during a short deployment, usually between 6 months and 1 year long. This is false, but understandable given that there are few genuinely helpful resources at the fingertips of deployers to help them understand and acquire the kind of language that may actually make a difference for them. The little beige military-oriented phrase books (available for Dari and Pashto) are one tool, but they begin with pages of phrases like "Don't shoot!" and "Put your hands in the air," which may well have application but are not often the phrases that will save the day.

The language-learning approach that worked well for us was firstly a highly relational one, prioritizing greetings and the phrases needed to facilitate continual language-learning. Next, it was not based on memorizing long vocabulary lists, but on listening for phrases that "punch above their weight" in terms of effect and significance, or their ability to lead to further learning. Finally, it was about being alert and prepared for seemingly small, but significant, opportunities to create human connections and communicate good intentions. I will briefly expand on each of these.

First, an effective language-learning approach in a counterinsurgency context is relational; learning the language becomes part of the process of engagement, rather than a prerequisite. This approach revolves around the recognition that the most natural and practical language-learning takes place in the context of daily life and tasks, by an active learner intentionally seeking out the company of native speakers—who in most cases tend to be very generous in helping newcomers learn. Have dinner with a linguist. Take a few minutes during a meeting with local officials or community leaders to ask about the history or folklore of the area. Ask a soldier in a partnered unit if he knows any poetry and what it is about.

Effective language learning also depends on the courageous humility of the language learner, knowing that he/she will make mistakes and "sound funny," but being willing to try out new phrases nevertheless. Because many do not bother to learn any language at all (to our shame), in Afghanistan the learner will usually find an abundance of grace, encouragement, and joy at his or her attempts to produce Dari or Pashto. Language-learning phrases like "What is this?" and "How do you say this in Dari/Pashto?" are the relational language-learner's best friend. These are "power-phrases" that are gateways to many more words, ideas, and conversations. They become power tools when we find memorable ways to embed the responses we hear into our minds. How embarrassing to ask for a word for something and then be unable to retain it for even five minutes! So knowing how to use the power-phrases as tools for language-learning is critical as well. For example, if I point at a book and say, *Een chi ast?* ("What's this?) and my Afghan friend says *kitab,* what do I say next? *Kitab?* Yes, *kitab*. So THIS (pointing) is *kitab?* Yes, *kitab!* Wow! Hey Mariam, did you know that this is *kitab?* Yes, that's right, *kitab*. This repetition gives my brain ample opportunity to correlate *kitab* to the object I was looking at or holding. Even better, I could stop and write down in a small notebook my anglicized version of *kitab* and draw a rough sketch.

The second (and related) aspect of basic COIN-oriented language-acquisition is that it should not be based on vocabulary-memorization or focused on trying to read or write right away. Our team found great success in listening for phrases that carry unexpected significance, and focusing on learning those. Every language contains certain phrases that carry more meaning than simple translations reveal. These too are powerful tools for both language-learning and engagement. In Dari and Pashto many of these words have to do with courtesy and hospitality, or are related to spirituality and religion. Proverbs and short poems are also very meaningful and an excellent investment of limited language-learning time.

For example, when hosted at the house or office of an Afghan colleague who has prepared a meal, when the food is served a gracious thing to say is *Zahmat kashideyn,* which means "You went to so much trouble!" This is a simultaneously an acknowledgement of the generosity of the host and a signal that the guest is tuned in to what hospitality means in the culture. Likewise, when the dinner or meeting is wrapping up, the guest may use the phrase *Ba ejaazayetaan,* meaning "by your permission," to seek the host's blessing to leave. This phrase is likewise a gracious way to excuse oneself in case of some interruption like a phone call. Even if everything else is in English or through a translator, phrases like these punctuate interactions with a courtesy and respect that leaves a distinctly positive impression.

The final aspect to language-learning for engagement effectiveness is preparing for opportunities to create human connections and goodwill. This can be done through basic conversational tools such as the "FORTE" approach used in language training for Afghan Hands. They practice being able to respond to basic questions about **family, occupation, recreation, transportation, and education (FORTE).** This is something military members can work on with unit linguists, and facilitates being able to give a short personal introduction. Here is a story of how this approach reaped dividends in the Afghan community during engagement at an Afghan girls' school.

Language Story: Elementary Hospitality

On the first day of Afghan Hands language immersion, Colonel Kirk and his battle buddy, Lieutenant Colonel Max Moore, were wearing their military uniforms for their introduction to their hosts, including an Afghan Corps engineer. The engineer later took Colonel Kirk along with his construction team to a site where a new elementary school was under construction across the street from the current facility. Colonel Kirk recounts the events that followed:

> When we arrived at the building site I learned that the project was a new school for the local neighborhood. I began to speak with the Afghan construction crew, who were shocked to see an American officer speaking Dari. Soon the group around me grew larger and locals began to invite me to their homes for dinner and to meet their neighbors. Soon an older gentleman asked my name. "Timur," I said, and he seemed very pleased by my Dari (as limited as it was), as well as my adopted Afghan name.
>
> I learned that he was the lead teacher at the school, and that the other men were on the staff. The engineer and I were invited to follow them, and after an affirming nod from the engineer, one man took me by the hand and led me through a grove of trees (I literally mean "by the hand" as in the sort of way that we American males find uncomfortable, but my cultural training kicked in, and I survived).
>
> The gentleman led us into the female principal's

office where, after introductions and tea, the head teacher directed my attention to a photo on the wall. "Do you know who this is?" he asked. I replied, "Yes—that is hero of Afghanistan, Ahmad Shah Massoud." You could hear a pin drop. They listened intently as I told them how I knew about Massoud, after which one of the staff presented me with a large poster of Massoud he had spontaneously produced. I accepted their gift and thanked them, expecting it to be our parting moment.

Instead, the gentleman and the principal led the engineer and me into a classroom of about 25 young girls in or around the fifth grade. The students stood up as we entered, and the principal told them, "This is our friend, Timur, from America. He is here to help the people of Afghanistan and wants to meet you all." She then indicated that I had the floor.

My heart raced from this surprise public speaking moment, but training kicked in once more as I recalled a short speech we had practiced. I told them about my family and my home, how I respected the people of Afghanistan and I hoped my country could help them. I ended by saying that I would like very much if we could become friends. Hands went over hearts all around the room as glowing smiles erupted. I thanked them and we exited.

I was relieved that I had seemed to survive my first speech in Afghanistan without too much embarrassment, but that relief was short-lived. The principal escorted us down the hall into the next classroom, and the scene was repeated for the next grade of young girls. This went on until I had spoken with most, if not all of the classes, probably some 250 students total.

There was only one awkward moment when a student asked me about Islam and my own faith. The staff began to rebuke her for asking this, but I replied in Dari, "I am a man of the Book, *ahl-e kitab*." The tension immediately turned to an even warmer reception than before. Thankfully, my Dari instructor had told me to anticipate such a question, so I was ready to explain.

We left the school in the most heartfelt scene I could ever hope to see. The students and teachers all lined up along the path leading from the school to say goodbye. As we were leaving, the principal stood atop the stairs and shouted to me as we walked back down the path, "It is very good that you have come here to see these children! You must tell your family that we are very grateful! We know that they are worried about you, but you must tell them that we will never allow any harm to come to you! Do you hear me?! PROMISE ME that you will tell your mother that we will never allow any harm to come to you because you are our friend!!"

I have never been an overly emotional guy, but I will never forget the honor I felt that day. The choked-up kind of honor that makes you wonder how to say in Dari, "No, I'm fine—just something in my eye."[40]

On Culture: Walls Have Reasons

Effective outreach and engagement is impossible without some level of cross-cultural aptitude. Hundreds of books and articles expound on its importance, but what does that mean practically in a place like Afghanistan? Both sides tend to erect barriers, whether mental or physical, to keep their "comfort zones" intact. These include physical walls, gates, and policies that make it difficult to make meaningful contacts in the first place. They also include a variety of attitudes, stereotypes, and preconceptions that keep both sides distant from each other. Afghans may be friendly, curious, indifferent, or hostile, but in almost all cases still need to be convinced through individual interactions that they can trust U.S. and coalition intentions: that they can trust a "foreign soldier." Effective cross-cultural communication is often the key to overcoming these walls, seeing doors open rather than applying any force.

Walls always exist for a reason. In a presentation to West Point cadets about the concept of "female engagement" in Afghanistan, I used the phrase "walls have reasons" to launch a discussion about honor, boundaries, and successfully overcoming cultural differences, whether perceived or real. Part of this discussion was about the practice of veiling, which in essence means erecting a portable wall. For an outsider or foreigner, choosing whether or not to veil was about the process of deconstructing or bypassing artificial walls (having to do with initial perceptions, preconceptions, and assumptions) by respecting real boundaries. Here are some of the "reasons" for boundaries or barriers that one might observe in Afghan culture:

- Physical walls around homes accentuate the significance of hospitality, the importance of loyalty and family ties.

- Treasuring privacy means keeping an appropriate distance between public and private spaces.

- For the more conservative members of Afghan society, maintaining the values of honor and modesty means keeping "mobile walls" (veils/burqas) between men and women (who are not each others' close relatives).

Once we began to understand what kinds of issues were most important to our Afghan colleagues and what gestures might make a difference, our team found that we could give certain recognized signs of respect, thereby demonstrating the effort to understand and the choice to honor boundaries. As we learned how to do this, we could build trust more rapidly and found we were able to get directly to the heart of things—and the heart of people. As described in previous sections, one monumentally effective way to begin breaking down these barriers is through language. The sections below describe some of the most significant areas of cultural interaction where our team found opportunities to show respect through recognized gestures and practices, leading to the dissolution of barriers and the growth of deep trust.

Since particulars of language and culture in a country as rich and diverse as Afghanistan vary significantly, observations should rarely be taken as a rigid rule. Whether interacting with Afghans outside or inside the walls of our compounds, the mindset itself is vastly more important than a list of do's and don'ts listed in a pamphlet, handbook, or online training. If we could win trust and communicate effectively in the cross-cultural space simply by refraining from showing the bottoms of our feet, it would be pretty simple.

Instead, cross-cultural communication is often about the intangibles. Most Afghans have not lived in a technology-intensive environment, and thus their skills at oral communication and reading the cues of human interaction are usually more highly-attuned than ours. It is sometimes as if they can read your mind and intentions from far away, before a conversation even begins. That makes the concept of clear intentions—*Niat-e saaf, manzele aasaan ("Clear intentions, easy destination")*—all the more critical. Many blunders will be forgiven if your intentions are honest, and discernible as such!

Below are some of the lessons we learned about how to make those intentions resonate in real life: what kinds of gestures and actions speak loudest in the Afghan cultural context. By these means we disrupt the enemy's intent to separate us from the people—and win in the psychological realm.

Culture Notes: Being a Good Guest

Honor the guest, O son.
Even though he be an infidel, open the door.

~Afghan Proverb

A common story is told to Afghan children:

> A group of thieves one night entered a man's house while all of the family was asleep. The thieves, under the instructions of their leader, began carrying out carpets and cushions - anything portable that had any worth. In the dark, the leader of the band reached into a cupboard, finding a hard smooth rock-like object. He immediately decided that it must be some kind of a gem. The thieves had almost finished their work when the leader put this "gem" to his lips. Tasting it, he was not only disappointed at finding that the gem was just a block of salt, but he was horrified that he had stolen the property of a man whose salt he had [tasted]. He immediately ordered his men to return all of the property to the house before the family awoke.[41]

This story shows how powerful the tradition of *naan wa namak* (bread and salt) is—a cultural phenomenon that may not have a modern-day equivalent in Western cultures. Partaking of the "salt" of our Afghan neighbors and partners, and sharing our salt with them, while acknowledging the significance of this act, is a powerful means of strengthening bonds so that cultural mistakes, mishaps, or other contentious issues do not have the power to tear them down.

Being a good guest certainly goes beyond partaking of food or drink at someone's house or office. There are many ways to be good "guests" in the country of Afghanistan as U.S. and coalition military members, including the way we drive, how we behave and dress in public, and so forth. But the importance of hospitality-contexts for building genuine trust and relationships should not be underestimated.

Three stories from our team's experience serve to illustrate the extraordinary hospitality of Afghans and opportunities to respond to that hospitality in culturally meaningful ways.

Story #1: Promoting Partnership

It was August, 2011, during Ramazan. Governor Saba, of the western province of Herat, had laid out an extravagant feast for the daily *iftaar* or "breaking of the fast," inviting our whole contingent to join him at his compound. The occasion? A promotion ceremony for the lead Afghan Hand in our organization, Colonel Kirk. A close friend, Dr. Davood Moradian, had helped arrange the event, and my task was to plan and narrate a ceremony that would be meaningful and symbolic, in an unknown place and in multiple languages, with guests including senior American and Afghan officials as well as Afghan civil society leaders.

After a lavish dinner, we commenced with the unusual ceremony, playing both national anthems as the official party processed into the Governor's receiving hall, where American and Afghan flags stood before a majestic painting of the historic "Minaret of Jam." The commander of ISAF's anti-corruption task force, Army MG H.R. McMaster officiated the ceremony, re-administering the oath of office, while Governor Saba and Dr. Moradian pinned Colonel Kirk's new rank on his uniform, according to military tradition.

Much to the audience's shock, Colonel Kirk made his entire speech in Dari, including words from the Persian poet Saadi, and asking me to "translate" (back into English). Using the words of the poem, he acknowledged the kindness of our hosts, and explained how normally for an event like a promotion ceremony one's family is present to celebrate. Here we were far away from our families, and yet a new family had stepped in and shown us an extravagant level of warmth and human care. The effect in the audience was profound. The General, Colonel Kirk and a few others even stayed the night at the Governor's house, and it was clear that the evening and its ceremony had promoted more than officer's rank; it had promoted a deep and genuine friendship.

At the Governor's House

Story #2: A Ten-Year Anniversary

While America was commemorating the tenth year after September 11th, many in Afghanistan were remembering Sept 9th, 2001. On that day, just before the deadly attack that would suddenly and painfully draw America's attention back to the troubled country of Afghanistan, a fiercely independent hero of the Afghan struggle against the Soviets, Ahmad Shah Massoud, was assassinated by a supposed journalist.

Huge blown-up posters with classic images of Massoud in prayer, Massoud with his field radio, Massoud reflecting over a book, were displayed everywhere along the road from Kabul to the Panjshir Valley. Our host, political figure and opposition leader Dr. Abdullah Abdullah, had invited a small group of us to pay our respects at the grave of Afghan leader and warrior who in 1998 wrote a letter to the American people "in the name of more than one and a half million Afghan martyrs who sacrificed their lives to uphold some of the same values and ideals shared by most Americans and Afghans alike."[42]

After stopping at Dr. Abdullah's garden for enormous plates of fresh fruit and milk-tea, we arrived at the famous hill where we dismounted the vehicles and walked up toward the shrine. A crowd of several thousand Panjshiris and devotees surged with us up the road packed with cars and motorcycles bearing black flags of mourning. Our small team walked among them, including the only American uniform (our colonel) and the only female present at the event (me). We paid our respects and returned to a different garden, where we were treated to more fruit and tea, followed by an lavish meal of meat and Qabuli palau (the traditional Afghan rice dish), served to the entire entourage of dozens of Pashtuns from Kandahar (where Abdullah's father is from) and Tajiks from the Panjshir (where Abdullah's mother is from). We were incorporated into the proceedings with graciousness and care, knowing that several of Abdullah's men were specifically assigned to preside over our physical security, and several others were to ensure that we ate a sufficient number of grapes and peaches!

Toward the end, we had the opportunity to present Dr. Abdullah with a gift on behalf of our commander, General McMaster, in appreciation of his hospitality. (This is a customary thing to do, but often the guest leaves the gift in a subtle way, putting it on a table or handing it to the host on the side, lest the host protest that it is enough of an honor just to have you as a guest.) It was a book of pictures that painted the great potential of Afghanistan, from the eager eyes of its youth and students, to fertile agricultural lands, to its mines and jewels. Here, the gesture served as an opportunity to express good wishes for Afghanistan and the future relationship between our nations, and Dr. Abdullah responded with emotion and earnest agreement.

The value of these encounters was hard to measure, as it ranged from the interactions with the hosts and other guests during the meal times, to the impressions created by walking and paying respects to Massoud on a significant day among the people. Without this gracious offer of hospitality and our ability to receive it as guests, the day's journey and meaningful exchanges would have been impossible.

Story #3: Lunch with the Taliban

Our team was invited to attend a conference organized by Afghan civil society leaders that brought together all kinds of Afghan civic leaders from around the country. One of our team members joined a friend from Helmand province at the buffet, then began looking for an available place to sit. The American was in civilian clothes, yet still stood out as a foreigner. Scanning the venue, he noticed one table with several empty seats, the remaining seats occupied by four rough-looking men who looked like they had stepped straight off a Taliban recruiting poster. The men were older, and likely old *mujahideen* affiliates, and were staring holes in him.

Our partner had found his desired seat—with an added challenge. He asked in Dari if he could have permission to join them for lunch. One glowered and responded (in Dari), "We don't speak Dari!" The others chuckled. Our man discerned these men were proud Pashtuns, and although he did not speak much Pashto, he knew his friend from Helmand did. "No problem," he replied in Dari. "My friend here is from Helmand and speaks Pashto. He will tell me how to ask for your permission." The Helmandi friend smiled and whispered to the American, who then repeated in broken Pashto what he'd heard. The rough-looking Afghans stared at each other incredulously, and the eldest-looking among them nodded and motioned for the men to sit down.

Conversation proceeded somewhat haltingly, with the American's Dari transmitted into whispered Pashto then repeated. Amused by the effort, the Afghans finally relented and switched to Dari. After customary pleasantries, the American asked where the men were from. One snorted the name of a village in Nangarhar, while another gruff voice added, "That's near *Tora Bora,*" intending to emphasize the notorious place where Osama bin Laden had fought Americans and narrowly escaped capture. The first Afghan continued, "It would be *very* dangerous for *you* to come to *my* village."

The American paused at the slightly veiled threat, then smiled as he sensed a cultural opportunity. "Not if I was your guest. If I was your guest, no harm would come to me." At this reply, the Afghans exchanged uncomfortable glances—how could it be that this foreigner understood *Pashtunwali?* Finally the first Afghan respectfully replied, "That is right. If you were my guest, you would be safe." The American smiled and handed the Afghan his business card saying, "And if you come to my country, you will be my guest, and I promise you will be safe." The hostility devolved into curiosity as the Afghans gazed at the card, puzzled by this disarming hospitality.

Later, the group asked our teammate why Americans were in Afghanistan. He replied, "The Prophet Sulaiman (King Solomon) has written that 'a gentle answer turns away wrath.' We are America's gentle answer." The Afghans nodded approvingly. By the end of lunch, the Afghan men had extended warm invitations to visit Nangarhar, as hugs and handshakes were exchanged and the elder Afghan said, "Today I will tell my whole family about you. I still can't believe that you are an American."

Culture Notes: Being a Good Host

While much outreach and engagement takes place beyond the walls, where it is imperative for ISAF personnel to conduct themselves as good guests, a critical component of outreach takes place inside the walls. Hosting Afghans on ISAF compounds presents a unique set of opportunities and challenges, and easily communicates to the guests whether or not the hosts have done their homework—the equivalence of showing respect.

In Afghanistan, the quality of a guest's experience establishes the character of the host. A good leader must be a generous host. A well-known proverb goes, *Bedune dastarkhwan khan neist!* "There is no leader (or khan) without [his] tablecloth," meaning the hospitable spread for guests. While Afghans recognize that customs differ in other countries, recognizing and honoring the guest-host relationship as it exists in Afghanistan is a powerful means for military leaders and outreach teams to inspire confidence and goodwill.

Skillful hosting is one of the most effective ways to deepen ISAF's relationships with the Afghan community, create positive and lasting impressions, work together on complex problems in a relaxed and secure manner, and dispel harmful rumors about what takes place within ISAF bases. By inviting Afghans to "share our salt," we make a contract of loyalty and friendship. The more we fine-tune our cross-cultural acumen by learning the art of gracious hosting, seeking to understand and genuinely embrace this process of bonding, the more effective we will be in the Afghan environment.

Because hosting is effort-intensive on the part of the military personnel, I have structured this section to include detailed, highly practical notes. Collected from hosting hundreds of meetings and events over the course of two years, the following are a few best practices and ideas on hosting Afghans on U.S. or coalition compounds.

Meeting Place and Amenities

Every base should have a reception and hosting area appropriate for Afghan guests. Disturbingly, many bases having nothing of the sort, or use an area that is clearly an afterthought. Few military personnel are trained in the art of hospitality, or realize its significance. In a place like Afghanistan this can be catastrophic, but thankfully it is not difficult to learn. The hospitality room should be among the best cared-for and highest quality facilities on base. This sends a message and Afghans will notice. Afghan homes place a high priority on their guest-reception area, because this is the first impression any outsider will get of the hosts. Whether a shura/jirga center, restaurant, conference room, or office, Afghans will notice whether hosts have taken care to prepare, which is far more important than the color of the tea or the fanciness of the carpets.

If possible, have snacks or sweets already laid out or readily available to serve, and tea ready to serve shortly after arrival. If a meal is planned, have tea ready to serve before and after, time allowing. Green tea with cardamom is widely appreciated, but again it is the thought—the intent demonstrated through action—that counts, not whether the tea was perfect. Obviously, still aim for perfection.

If it is a first meeting, tea with snacks is generally more than suitable. Still, it is always better to have more than just enough, even if it is just dried fruit and cookies. If you have leftovers, a good practice is to send them with the guests or give them to gate guards or day laborers. The treatment of these often-forgotten daily "guests" on our compounds translates into the base's relationship with the surrounding community.

Reception

Ensure guests are given clear directions to the place where they will be received and meet their hosts (likely outside the gates); this step is often forgotten and can lead to a sour beginning if it is ignored. Often those living inside a base are not familiar with local names for surrounding streets or landmarks. Ensure guests have at least one phone number they can call if lost, preferably of someone with superior Dari/Pashto and familiarity of the gates and surrounding areas.

When welcoming guests, greet profusely and clearly explain process and rules for entering the base. If searches are required, hosts should voluntarily undergo the same procedures whenever feasible, and ask for the guest's forgiveness for the inconvenience.

Hosting Teams

Whenever possible, have a separate person or team from those escorting preparing the area where the meeting and/or meal will take place. Greet guests at the door, as if you have been waiting for them all day. Show them in, preferably to places farthest from the door. A good phrase to use is *baalaa bishineyd,* or "sit higher," indicating a place of honor.

If possible, assign one or two people (or more based on the size of the group) to "fuss" over the needs of the guests. Don't ask if they need more tea; pour it. Ask, "More cake?" as you are serving them another slice. Insist. If there is an ISAF leader who is expected but has not yet arrived, ensure the guest knows he/she is held up but sends greetings and apologies and is coming as quickly as possible.

Other Courtesies

If you are just serving tea or light snacks, such as for a first meeting, express the desire to meet again when they can be your guests for a "proper" meal. If you have been their guest before, think of it as a "hospitality competition;" whether it is pizza or pancakes or pilau, make sure it is plentiful.

While artificial constraints such as additional meetings may exist, traditionally the guest asks permission of the host to go, while the host insists the guests stay as long as they would like. In Dari, the phrase to use is *ba ejazayetaan* ("by your permission"), or *ejaaza ast?* ("is there permission?") Often the host uses the Dari phrase *Shau bosheyn*, meaning "Please stay the night!" The guest does not (usually) accept this generous offer, but offering demonstrates that the host considers the guest's presence an honor, not an inconvenience.

Culture Notes: To Veil or Not to Veil?

*Hijab protects the family and...the woman
from being viewed as a sexual object.*

~Umm Mohammad Biadon, Women's Rights
Activist, Southern Lebanon

In addition to customs and courtesies revolving around hospitality, another major area that presents an opportunity to demonstrate cultural acumen and respect is the issue of modesty, specifically female head-covering.

Emotions often ran high on both sides in discussions about whether female U.S. military members should wear headscarves in uniform. From the quote above, one can deduce that there are many different views of the functions and usefulness of the veil or "hijab." After operating in daily engagement with Afghan people in a variety of contexts: workplaces, homes, government offices, and on the street, I would *not* argue that all military females should wear scarves at all times. However, it is reasonable for that decision to fall to the lowest-level (tactical) leader involved in the actual operations impacted by the decision.

I sought to cover my head on most occasions outside coalition bases, and I believe this made me more effective as a female professional working in Afghanistan. It removed many artificial barriers (stereotypes, distractions), allowing our team to make genuine connections and build trust more quickly. In most cases, covering my head was a means of observing an important boundary for many women there: between me, as a woman, and *their* men. For a small number of city-dwelling Afghan women this boundary did not matter nearly as much; in fact there were some who themselves did not generally cover their heads and certainly preferred Western women not to. This was a very small minority, but in some cases it was not appropriate to veil and would have been awkward to do so.

The issue of veiling has become highly politicized in many regions of the world, as the spectrum of conservative to modern expressions of Islam contend for socio-political space. This book does not seek to address the complexities of the subject, such as the ways veiling has sometimes been used as a tool of oppression and subjugation, even becoming a symbol for it, as in the case of Afghanistan's blue "burqa" or *chadri*. Advocates of women's rights in places like Afghanistan are engaged in a battle for respect: the right to be acknowledged and treated as equal human beings, the right to be both seen and heard in the public sphere without harassment. I write this with deep esteem for and dedication to this cause. However, I argue that the issue of head-covering for military members serving in Afghanistan is of an entirely different nature. It is our choice to cover or not cover our heads, and in many cases the decision to do so was honoring to both male and female Afghans present. There is nothing inherently evil about a headscarf, as it can tastefully express style, modesty, and femininity. The vice is in compulsion and harassment, rather than in a piece of cloth. With that in mind, I focus this discussion on why decisions on whether military females should veil or not veil in uniform should be made by those women (who are actually engaging with Afghans) and their leadership at the lowest possible level.

While received with great warmth by most Afghans, my efforts at cultural respect were not always understood or approved by military command. One day, after a high-profile event where I wore a headscarf, a senior commander at NTM-A ordered me never to wear a headscarf in uniform again. I then had to be creative to find other ways to cover appropriately—so as to still be effective and respectful. One of my teammates discovered a piece of issued military gear—a balaclava-style fire hood—that could be used as a type of "tactical headscarf." The wearer could not be considered out of uniform since the gear was issued, while the intended effect was still achieved: to demonstrate understanding and respect for the Afghan context, simultaneously deconstructing harmful stereotypes about Westerners and Western females in particular.

Below I outline several principles to explain the reasoning behind our team's approach to the wearing the headscarf in Afghanistan:

Clothing is communication. Taking off a glove to shake a hand, removing shoes at the appropriate time, and wearing a headscarf are all ways of communicating through attire. If I, by donning a piece of cloth, can convey respect and humility and simultaneously work to dismantle a toxic stereotype of Americans, why would I not do so? The simple gesture means something to another and costs me nothing. While I do not presume to speak for the feelings and opinions of all Afghans, in my experience almost every time I have worn the headscarf in uniform, the response of both Afghan women and men was overwhelmingly positive.

Professionalism. Some headscarves worn in uniform admittedly have not portrayed the right image; flashy, patterned, or brightly colored fabrics are probably not the right answer for military professionals. Instead, beige, black, grey, sage, or other appropriately shaded scarves can be worn, demonstrating respect both for the host culture and the time-honored traditions of the uniform. Female members of the Afghan National Army and Police pull it off quite gracefully.

Practicality. A headscarf need not interfere with the function of any piece of military headgear or uniform item. Headscarves worn in military uniform can be clean-cut and easy to take on and off without hassle. The model I used actually came from Iraqi friends in Tucson, Arizona and requires zero "fussing." It kept my hair out of my eyes and the dust out of my hair. I wore it under helmet and cover alike. And when I was prohibited to wear a headscarf, the alterable balaclava served similar practical functions.

Forbidding and mandating are equally oppressive...and foolish. The answer is not to mandate OR prohibit the wearing of "hijab" in deployed settings. One only has to read the history of Iran's forced prohibition and then compulsory reinstatement of the veil to realize that such extremes are not helpful. Commanders and supervisors at the lowest levels should make decisions about the headscarf based on tactical as well as personal considerations, but policy can and should clarify the professional parameters and procedures for wear. When my supervisors and I had the freedom to adapt to the environment and its variables (as we did on the anti-corruption task force), we were most effective.

Mission Effectiveness/Security. Our greatest assets or "weapon" in civil engagement and outreach are not the armored vehicle or M-4 rifle. They are language, culture, and the resulting ability to connect effectively. When this ability is compromised, so is the mission. The physical image we present can communicate cultural understanding or the lack thereof, which impacts the rest of the interaction. While driving and walking around the city, I felt much safer wearing a headscarf, drawing less negative attention, and perhaps even drawing positive attention instead. The simple act of wearing a tasteful, appropriate headscarf set a positive tone for countless meetings that led to significant relationships and partnerships.

In the case of American military females, the "chador" issue needn't be skewed, as some have implied, to be about females being treated as "second class" soldiers or citizens. We should strive for a level of nuance that recognizes the headscarf as more than a religious accouterment or symbol of female oppression. While forced covering is oppressive, there are many women who see head-covering as a core part of their identity and culture.

The question of covering the head is emblematic of a variety of cross-cultural quandaries. Trust is built on a foundation of mutual respect, and that respect does not stem from stubbornly clinging to our own cultural norms but rather discovering actions that effectively bridge the gap. For women, perhaps this entails wearing an extra piece of material. For men, perhaps it is overcoming inhibitions about holding hands with or kissing another male on the cheek in greeting. A mature, balanced level of cultural adaptation shows strength, not weakness. This does not mean "becoming them" or "going native" but rather finding touch-points, ways of demonstrating thoughtfulness and appreciation that break down otherwise stubborn barriers.

Ultimately, simple gestures demonstrate that we're listening; they cost us nothing and yet are priceless in terms of demonstrating respect and appreciation without compromising or pandering. And the main power of the gesture is the intention: we do this of our own free will.

Author with Afghan Policewomen

For the Non-Military Reader

I was surprised to find so much distinguished talent among the citizens and so little among the heads of the government. It is a constant fact that at the present day the ablest men...are rarely placed at the head of affairs.

~Alexis de Tocqueville, "Democracy in America," 1835

Much of this short volume was designed to be especially relevant for a military audience and those connected to them. Yet the role of citizens in the battle we are fighting is desperately important. A first step for citizens keen to be informed and involved is to tune in, as you have done by reading this book, to voices and perspectives other than the conventional media. U.S. political leaders have failed to explain to the American public the national interests at stake and cast a vision for what is possible with resolve, consistency, and creativity. These chapters have elucidated, albeit briefly, the bumbling attempts of large bureaucracies to engage effectively. That's where everyday citizens come in. While this author acutely hopes that the nation's leaders and those steering its military and diplomatic bureaucracies will adjust course, it is citizens who must realize that outcomes affect all of us and demand these changes. It is citizens who are free to inform themselves, to act with independence and creativity.

The recognition of the importance of the role and perspective of citizens, whether Afghans, Americans, or others, is what led me, along with a small team, to establish the nonprofit Civil Vision International (CVI). CVI seeks to connect citizens to each other and to stories beyond the headlines, especially of individuals and groups doing visionary work. It's easy to support and get involved in this process—as simple "liking" the Facebook page and beginning to share content you find compelling. Social networking is an increasingly powerful way to stay informed, make new, meaningful connections, and spread ideas.

While we at Civil Vision International cherish face-to-face interactions and wish we could sit down with you for a long chat over green tea with cardamom, we're excited by the potential for real world impact through social media. If you'd like to do something about what you've read in this book, challenge it, or meet others who are also thinking about these issues, we'd be thrilled to see you on one of our sites. As a starting-point, here are some places you can go:

- Free App for iPhone and Android: search for Civil Vision
- Facebook: search Civil Vision International
- Twitter handle: @civil_vision
- YouTube channel: CivilVision
- Instagram: civilvision
- Tumblr: civilvision
- Wordpress blog: http://afghanistanvisionnetwork.wordpress.com/

If you have any trouble or have ideas you want to share, please write to civilvisioninternational@gmail.com. We can't do it without you and we mean that.

Conclusion(s):

READ CAREFULLY BEFORE PROCEEDING

This is not your average, tidy conclusion. But to win wars (and hearts), some rules must be broken. What follows are three conclusions, of which you may choose to read only one. So, choose carefully. If you are policy-making or academically oriented, you may want to choose conclusion #1. If you are a soldier, military leader, or directly concerned about or involved in winning our nation's wars, skip the first and read conclusion #2. If you are more of an artist or a poet, I suggest you skip the first two and choose conclusion #3. (I know you might break the rules and read more than one conclusion, for which you will be forgiven. Refer to beginning of this paragraph.)

Conclusion #1

When Dr. Niazi said that the hearts of the Afghan people are for sale, "but not for money," he illuminated the key to rectifying both our view and our approach to the conflict in Afghanistan. A visionary, winning strategy in Afghanistan is within reach; it must be one that recognizes the nature and high stakes of the conflict, focuses on the pivotal importance of the human, psychological dimension, and embraces a humble supportive role through listening to Afghan counterparts. Success demands a rejection of bureaucratic lethargy and inflexibility, requiring instead the careful selection of civil servants and military leaders who are capable of building relationships, trust, and creative solutions rather than higher walls for secure compounds. Honest and transparent engagement with the American people is likewise crucial, presenting realistic goals and offering means for American citizens to be informed and involved. These are not new lessons; they are historic ones that we have forgotten—or never learned in the first place.

The conflict we face in Afghanistan is part of an old and existential struggle between those who believe in the subjugation and oppression of people, whether couched in ideological, political, or religious terms, and those who hold to the principles of human dignity and freedom. It is a struggle our nation has encountered before, and when the Greatest Generation laced up their boots to face it, the American people could feel in their bones the necessity of doing battle with destructive ideologies like Nazism and other forms of fascism. The fight was a highly conventional one—something our military understood well—and the price paid by those who fought and those who loved them alike was astronomical. These sacrifices, though incomprehensibly great, were recognized as honorable and crucial.

Our nation again faced this struggle in Vietnam. There we recognized the threat posed by Vietcong totalitarianism and facilitated by communist ideology, but we failed to recognize the human, psychological, and political nature of the conflict. U.S. policymakers took an overwhelmingly limited conventional military approach and allowed the enemy to have a safe haven, a capable sponsor, and space to woo the people with a sinister vision of the future, veiled in appealing nationalism. In this situation, we needed creative, people-oriented solutions focused on partnering with and strengthening the resolve of the Vietnamese people to realize their own positive vision, while simultaneously denying the enemy safe haven and support. Supposedly small matters like governmental legitimacy and corruption were left to fester amidst the people as we failed to listen to them. While Afghanistan's history, culture, and context are distinct from those of Vietnam, the principal issues are remarkably similar.

These ideas emerge compellingly in Rufus Phillips' *Why Vietnam Matters: An Eyewitness Account of Lessons Not Learned*. Phillips explains the reasons for U.S. failure in Vietnam, pointing out how we did not know ourselves, we did not understand our South Vietnamese allies, and we knew even less about North Vietnam. Compounding these handicaps, however, "Absolutely fatal was the failure to explain openly and honestly to the American people what the war was about and what we were trying to achieve."[43] The absence of critical understanding, especially of our allies and enemies in Vietnam, stemmed from a fixation on "numbers," impoverished engagement, and a failure to listen. Today we ignore these lessons to our own peril.
Now the conflict in Afghanistan hangs in the balance.

If we want to win hearts and wars, we must *listen.*

*Wall Art at Afghanistan New Generation
Organization in Kabul*

Conclusion #2

The stakes in Afghanistan are extremely high, and the sacrifices have been immense. The victory, too, can be great, if we apply some hard-core American resolve, creativity, and leadership. To win, we must name the enemy, identifying and rejecting his messages. We must get serious about listening to the Afghan people (the "good guys") and getting and staying close to them, which is exactly what the enemy does NOT want us to do. And we must not give up.

We cannot effectively face our enemy in Afghanistan until we name him: the duplicitous Pakistani ISI and their extremist fighters, trained (brainwashed), armed and equipped in Pakistan. The Taliban, among other groups, are not an indigenous insurgency but are pawns used to project foreign Pakistani power and interests in Afghanistan, at great cost to American and international soldiers as well as the Afghan people.

Our enemy is motivated by totalitarian ideology shrouded in the religious language of Islamic extremism, who seeks to destroy not just Afghanistan, but our own freedom and way of life. We should not be duped into thinking that this fight will end with our peaceful "transition" (i.e. retreat) from Afghanistan. If we don't finish the job, our defeat and withdrawal will turn Afghanistan into the world's largest salt-lick for Islamic nut-jobs, and it won't be long before a reinvigorated terror network strikes Europe and America with a vengeance. This is not fear-mongering. It is our enemy's stated intent. These extremists will not stop until our way of life is eradicated and replaced by a feudalistic fascism posing as religious piety.

So what do we do? Kill more? Hardly.

We can never kill enough bad guys to solve Afghanistan's problems, especially if we refuse to address the root of the problem in Pakistan. However, success in Afghanistan hinges on re-focusing on the "good guys" who are on our side, a powerful friendly force who has the most to lose if totalitarianism takes over. Many Afghans remain on the fence as a matter of survival, due to intimidation and the psychological war waged to great effect by the enemy against them and us. When Dr. Niazi said that the hearts of the Afghan people are for sale, "but not for money," he illuminated the key to winning this battle for hearts, which begins with recognizing the human, psychological dimension of the fight. It begins with *listening.*

The people are *not* the Afghan central government, which until now we have largely mistaken for the strategic goal, while opportunists and criminals there repeatedly played us like chumps. We have failed to see that the central government is only important because it affects the common people in every dimension of life, from security to governance to corruption. We have failed to understand the proper roles of civil society, the private sector, and the government that lead to stability and the rule of law. We cannot continue to mistake a "government" for "governance." We must realize that authentic development takes time and cannot be rushed, surged, or expedited with cash. We failed to listen to the Afghan people, but instead created a well-organized, well-heeled, highly corrupt institutional excuse for an Afghan government that hangs like a noose from our necks. Yet there is still time if we will only *listen.*

The "good guys" are everywhere in Afghanistan and are ready to help us win—but they need a safe haven, sponsorship, and most of all, vision. They are ordinary Afghan citizens, especially women and young people, who cannot flee to Europe or America with a dual-citizenship visa. Common people, so easily ignored with their quiet voices, constitute this war's strategic level of effort, and their backs are against the wall. The civil society groups that represent them are a strategic gold mine of insight, and yet our efforts to date have mostly ignored them. The Afghan people know the Taliban, the ISI, and the fascism they promote. These are the good people who, when empowered, will drive out the extremists. Their strength will crowd out the enemy's impunity. If you find this hard to believe, then I invite you to spend an hour with courageous students at universities around Afghanistan. They make this point crystal clear. Their vision will supersede the extremists' vision as it taps into the desires that Afghans, like people everywhere, have for their future: a place where their children can grow up in safety, free from oppression and the twin destitutions of poverty and war. But we must *listen* to them.

We must also recognize that the conflict we face in Afghanistan is part of an old and existential struggle between those who believe in the subjugation and oppression of people and those who hold to the principles of human dignity and freedom. It is a struggle our nation has encountered before, and when the Greatest Generation laced up their boots to face it, the American people could feel in their bones the necessity of doing battle with destructive ideologies like Nazism and other forms of fascism. The fight was a highly conventional one—something our military understood well—and the price paid by those who fought and those who loved them alike was astronomical. These sacrifices, as incomprehensibly great as they were, were recognized as honorable and crucial.

Our nation again faced this struggle in Vietnam. Although we recognized the threat posed by Vietcong totalitarianism facilitated by communist ideology, we failed to recognize the human, psychological, and political nature of the conflict. U.S. policymakers took an overwhelmingly limited conventional military approach and allowed the enemy to have a safe haven, a capable sponsor, and to communicate appealingly an unacceptable vision for the future. Only when creative, people-oriented solutions to partner with and strengthen the resolve of the Vietnamese people to realize their allied vision for the future could we hope to be successful, as we simultaneously denied the enemy a safe haven and their sponsor's capability to support them. Supposedly small matters like corruption and legitimacy were left to fester amidst the people as we failed to listen to them. The situation is essentially distinct in Afghanistan, but the principle issues are remarkably similar. This is a paradox of COIN. We ignore the repeated lessons to our own peril.

In *Why Vietnam Matters: An Eyewitness Account of Lessons Not Learned,* author Rufus Phillips explains the reasons for U.S. failure in Vietnam, pointing out how we did not know ourselves, we did not understand our South Vietnamese allies, and we knew even less about North Vietnam. Compounding these handicaps, however, "Absolutely fatal was the failure to explain openly and honestly to the American people what the war was about and what we were trying to achieve."[45]

A most important truth remains, one that the good Afghan people make very clear: none of our efforts matter so long as the enemy retains his vision, his safe haven, and his sponsors. It is high time we get serious about doing the job and doing it right—that's what Americans do—and that's rightfully what the Afghan people expect of us. The Good

Guys *want* us to win and want to take ownership—for the sake of their country. Yet the enemy is counting on us to be weak and to falter. The enemy expects us to give up and go home. The enemy truly *believes* that we will. So if we firmly resolve to act now, stick to our principles, and turn this game around with the Good Guys behind us—then *our enemy is right where we want him*. We can defeat him.

Winning in Afghanistan, like in Vietnam, is decidedly not about the numbers (troops, dollars, enemy casualties) which have monopolized the thinking of American policymakers and journalists, especially with regard to the "withdrawal" unscrupulously scheduled for 2014. This war is fought and won on a psychological battlefield—success is therefore found in the human dimension. Our weapons include culture, education, civil society empowerment, and *listening*. The scoreboard includes the feelings and perspectives of the Afghan people, and indeed those of the American people, without whose support the sacrifices and gains of the last decade will surely be in vain.

Hearts are for sale, but cannot be purchased with money. Hearts are not gained through the killing of bad guys alone. They are not wooed with slick messages or glossy strategic communication. Hearts are bought with genuine humility, respect, and legitimate results. Hearts are won by listening, performing and delivering tangible and *authentic* outcomes that serve the *authentic* needs, desires, and vision of the *authentic* Afghan people. To succeed in COIN we can never do better, nor should we think to do less.

There is no doubt. Together, we can still win. There is yet time. There is every reason to hold on to a Great Hope.

The Good Guys are still with us. They know what to do and how to do it. They are right there, living across the street from our high-walled hideouts. We are winning now, but do not understand: if we will only find them, join them, win their hearts rightly, and *listen.*

Conclusion #3

Consider a land of strange debris:
orchards of unpicked berries rotting under trees,
unopened envelopes bearing healing seeds
kick-tossed across parched fields by a mindless breeze,
med-conventions showcasing life-saving cures
with no way to inject,
containers piled with high-tech wires
but no way to connect.

Leave for a moment
what you think you know,
Absurdistan-glutted screens,
poison-spores spreading *retreat,*
defeat-speech borne by dragon seeds.

Listen instead
to unscreamed newborn screams,
to teenagers on balance beams,
to Strategist's and Shoeshine's
uninstructed dreams,
to frontier possibilities.

Seek men who do not crumble
when the heat throttles up,
don't give up gold to drink,
once safely home,
the participant's paper cup;
men not swayed by a throng
of somnolent hands,
who will not ransom peace
for a chest-full of clanking cans.

114

Seek women
wielding sentences like swords,
unwavering whether death
or freedom their reward,
who do not wallow
on the silent sidelines
but swallow bitter risk
for a chance to savor joy
and justice.

Will you gather order from rubble
or let your loss (of face) consume what's left?
Will you compose new art from broken glass
or let it tear your feet?
Will you turn this scattered story
into poem-polished prose
or will you let this Eden burn
and decompose?

Afterword: Reasons for Hope

As this book goes to press, reports of the latest inflammatory comments by President Karzai accusing the U.S. of conspiring with the Taliban and new tragic "green on blue" attacks threaten to drain already dissipating American resolve, piling more fuel on fires of confusion and distrust. While I know many who are unwaveringly optimistic about Afghanistan's future, I served with one leader who has a unique perspective on Afghanistan based on not only his years of service there, but his service in another conflict location—Korea. He has graciously provided insight here on why this comparison is apt—and should give us strong reasons for hope.

Reasons for Hope

by Tim Kirk

I find myself involved in many discussions on what victory looks like and what it means to "win" in Afghanistan. So many problems persist and worsen. Corruption and political chaos burden the people. The very government established by the international community violates human rights and seeks narrow political objectives. Relationships are strained and patience wears thin. Yet I am absolutely optimistic about Afghanistan's future. I firmly believe Afghanistan is capable of becoming both an economic power and a lighthouse of human rights and the rule of law. In addition to the compelling evidence I saw from two years serving among and beside the Afghan people, I draw on my experience on a different tour of duty—in a country that few people think of as "combat."

People are surprised when I explain that the U.S. still has some 28,000 troops deployed in South Korea, and that when I "deployed" there in 2002 those troops received the same combat entitlements we received in Afghanistan that year and receive today. Perhaps even more surprisingly, South Korea provides a relevant example of what victory in Afghanistan can and will look like one day.

Really? South Korea? Why does that matter? Well, few remember that in 1950 U.S. President Truman ordered troops to war in Korea alongside the international community amid a great deal of controversy in the face of tyrannical hostility. The National Security Council (which Truman chaired) had just signed off on the Chairman of the Joint Chiefs of Staff's recommendation saying that Korea was "of little strategic value to the United States and that commitment to United States use of military forces in Korea would be ill-advised." The international community later realized, however, that unchecked communist expansion in Asia meant new evil enforced upon millions of people.

An armistice in July of 1953 served as a cease-fire agreement that settled the political situation closer to the pre-war status quo, but a technical state of war exists to this day. America lost over 36,000 troops in less than three years of fighting from 1950-1953. These are sobering numbers when we consider the fractional losses of Afghan and international troops in a decade-long war against our mutual enemies in Afghanistan. The fighting was fierce, but the U.S. and its allies fostered hope and launched a generational nation-building effort that has produced remarkable results on the Korean Peninsula.

Before we look at these results, consider how much effort and time it took to achieve them. South Korea didn't hold a democratic national election until 1988, 35 years after the ceasefire opened the door to stability efforts. From 1953 until that time, there were great debates among international elites and intellectuals on whether the Korean people could even handle self-rule. Many so-called experts saw the Korean people as feudalistic, tribal, illiterate, and culturally incompatible with democracy and the rule of law. Korea had just emerged from decades of constant war that destroyed nearly every institution and over half the dwellings of the region. Millions died during the fighting of 1950-53, but that was after years of invasion and counter-invasion by regional powers that left many Koreans homeless and destitute. South Korea's capital city of Seoul was completely demolished. Schools, hospitals, and law enforcement agencies were virtually non-existent. Continued war loomed as North Korea continued political subterfuge and insurgent tactics in the south. Sound familiar at all?

The debates about authoritarian versus democratic systems from 1953-1988 took place amid ruthless, corrupt political regimes that used violence and intimidation instead of principled governance and the rule of law. Military juntas dominated national politics, and student opposition movements suffered through repression and murder at the hands of the government for decades before transparent and accountable systems were established. Through it all, good governance and the rule of law finally took hold. A country one-sixth the size of Afghanistan with despotic neighbors-on-the-border bent on their destruction eventually prevailed to become a model of democratic rule.

Today, South Korea has Asia's 4th largest GDP (PPP) and the 12th largest in the world. It is the capital of the world's semiconductor industry, and is the world's 5th largest automobile manufacturer. It is also the 5th largest consumer nation of American farm products. It was ranked 8th on Transparency International's 2011 corruption index in the Asia/Pacific region, and 43rd in the world (USA was 24th). South Korea hosted the 1988 Summer Olympic Games and will host the 2018 Winter Olympics, too. Even their cultural icons dominate global attention, with the innovative Korean tech firm Samsung leading world smartphone sales through their Galaxy S III/IV products, and Korean musician Psy achieving the most viewed video in YouTube history with "Gangnam Style"—a tribute to the namesake Korean neighborhood. South Korea even has troops deployed in support of ISAF in Afghanistan. That contentious international nation-building effort in Asia has produced remarkable results by nearly every measurement.

Yet America still spends many resources protecting South Korea over 60 years after the beginning of a war that technically continues today. Troops still receive hostile fire entitlements because thousands of artillery pieces and missile launchers in North Korea point at South Korea. When I was stationed there from 2002-2003, the North fired upon and sank a South Korean ship, as they continued offensive operations against U.S. forces. When I visited again in 2006, North Korea inflamed international controversy by allegedly testing a nuclear weapon. Today, the North's despotic regime plagues the world with large-scale monetary counterfeiting, nuclear proliferation, support for terrorism and ongoing threats toward South Korea and the international community. North Korea even now declares the armistice that ended the Korean War is null and void. The conflict is still low-intensity today, but the war undoubtedly continues. On any given day, things could quickly escalate to a catastrophe. In light of these facts, how can the media accurately describe Afghanistan as "America's longest war?"

When I talk with folks who are interested in Afghanistan, they often bring up costs and casualties (usually thinking that Afghanistan has been extraordinarily expensive in both). They are interested to learn that Afghanistan is actually a remarkable example of low-cost conflict in American history of war. For example, the total cost of the Korean War during fiscal years 1951-1953 was $752 billion in 2012 dollars, with a total military cost from 1951-2000 of $1.1 trillion.[46] According to the Center for Defense Information, the estimated cost of the war in Afghanistan 2001-12 was approximately $460 billion. So ten years in Afghanistan has been 40% cheaper than three years in Korea in military dollar-costs, but also resulted in fewer casualties. Every life lost is precious, and every death is tragic, but it is important to consider that in ten years the U.S. has lost some 1,600 troops to hostile enemy action. That means that the U.S. lost more troops during a single year in Korea than we've lost over a decade in Afghanistan.

That's a sobering comparison, but it really should not be about what we've lost, but what those losses mean and what they've achieved. The Afghan-international coalition has achieved remarkable results in Afghanistan in a relatively short time (e.g. two democratic elections in ten years vs. zero in Korea for 35 years). For a glimpse of those achievements, I recommend two books, *Come From the Shadows* by Terry Glavin, and *The Long Way Back* by Chris Alexander. I think you'll see that Afghan and international troops have sacrificed and given their lives in purchase of miraculous results for the Afghan people and the international community. We should honor those sacrifices by going forward. Surrendering Afghanistan to the aggression of extremists would render those achievements and sacrifices null and void—and will certainly invite an expansion of their tyrannical goals.

Hearts for Sale has given us a good idea of what coalition victory in Afghanistan looks like, and how Afghanistan and the international community can achieve it. Yet the example of South Korea, while it is by no means a one-to-one correlation, further illuminates these points. Perseverance, determination and resolve go a long way in achieving remarkable results in this kind of war. I get annoyed when I hear someone call Afghanistan "America's Longest War," so I remind them about South Korea. Our troops have been earning combat stripes in Korea a lot longer than they have in Afghanistan, but we owe it to them, our hosts, and ourselves in *both nations* to persevere until the job is done.

I believe that Afghanistan has even more in its favor than South Korea did in 1965, after a decade of international assistance. We should also be mindful that just like in Afghanistan, the remarkable gains in South Korea are fragile. North Korea is certainly not content to allow such prosperity and self-governance to continue. We must remain vigilant in both cases, and secure room for the power of freedom to grow. When we are old and gray, our children may yet see Afghanistan lead the world economically with good governance. I suggest we tell them of these darker days and of the few who believed in a bright Afghan future. We all need a reason for hope, and there is every reason to believe in Afghanistan.

© Tim Kirk 2013

Appendix A:
Words from Afghans

Excerpts from messages received upon leaving
Afghanistan, March 2010

While there are many ways to describe the results of our work, our team felt that the most meaningful measure came from the words of our Afghan colleagues. I share a few of their comments here.

"This is a sad news to see you departing after such a long standing work and endeavor for the betterment of our environment in Afghanistan. Thanks for your job, your beautiful farewell letter and for your commitment for our mutual cause. Looking forward to seeing you back sometimes in the near future. We will continue our mutual work. Hopefully nothing will be preventing us from the optimism that we have developed in the recent years."

~School Director

"Unfortunately I received the bad news of your [departure] from Afghanistan. My heart is always with you. Please remember Afghan Women who are the victims of dirty politics and violence for decades in the history of Afghanistan. We never forget people like you who helped Afghans from bottom of their heart."

~Afghanistan Parliamentarian

"It is truly unfortunate that a person as kind as you is leaving Afghanistan. Please always remember that your devoted colleagues the Afghans will never forget you. Afghans are a poor people but have an expansive heart! In hopes of seeing you in the future and wishing you success." *~Youth Leader*

"I really appreciate your talent and efforts in this country; all your efforts [have been] counted worthy and you will have our prayers, well wishes, and friendship with you."

~Afghan Businessman
(Translation from Dari)

"You [have always been] worthy and honorable, may God protect you. Your service and efforts, your integrity are an honor for the people of Afghanistan forever."

~Director, Leadership Institute

"We are working for a good cause, and we are not to lose the struggle.... I am sure you will be back with more energy and added courage and passion. A mountain cannot move to reach other mountain, but human beings besides being small in size –but great in creation –will do it. Thank you."

~Leader, Human Rights and Education Organization

"Getting acquainted with you has been a great honor. I have been touched with your sense of friendship and the love you have extended to us and our country. We should learn from you how to love Afghanistan. Thank you indeed, see you soon and wish to see you back soon."

~Civil Society Leader

"After the time we have known your sweet friendship, I believe that distance can only be physical not of the heart. One thing that should be acknowledged is that your place is one no other person can fill. Maybe there will be someone filling your position but the pain we feel because of your absence is forever.... I promise you that we will not forget you. With esteem and in hopes of seeing you."

~Civil Society Activist
(Translation from Dari)

"You are leaving after passing very productive moments with Afghans and for Afghans. I hope our ways will cross each other in the near future. Let's hope to have you back in Kabul! Warm regards,"

~Newspaper Editor

"It was really so difficult to believe that the day has come that I have received your letter bidding goodbye. I did not wish this day to come.... I loved the companionship with you at different meetings. I remember the day when we were newly introduced at ISAF HQ and we discussed things with the Anti-Corruption campaign.... Our mission of fighting corruption and bringing transparency to Afghanistan will continue but your absence will be felt always along the way. Sincerely,"

~CEO, Civil Society Organization

"Beloved sister, my wish for you and other heroic women like you is that we would have you again soon in our midst, to [continue] working for peace and democracy in Afghanistan. We are dismayed to be apart from you but have hope that you will not forget us. I give you a promise that I was and am a part of your team, and I am ready to serve anywhere and anytime you need me. All the best, we love you."

~Women's Activist
(Translation from Dari)

"As an Afghan woman [your letter] gives me the courage to go forward because we go the same journey. Thanks for your support and encouragement for Afghans and personally me during your mission in Afghanistan. I am waiting for the day that you returned back to your second home..."

~Leadership Trainer & Coach

"We the people of Afghanistan are pleased with you and always have with us the memories of you. Please be happy everywhere you go. Thank you."

~TV Producer

"Your work was inspirational to me, even though I saw you in person only one time. When I read your e-mail, my heart broke [that you were leaving]. But here's hoping you will return. With respect,"

~Youth Activist

"It was very nice to have you all that time. We won't forget you; you are with us all the time wherever you are. Distances can't affect on the strong relations was created among you and all Afghans. I appreciate your efforts and all you did for Afghanistan and for the people of this country…"

~Law professor and CEO of Legal Consulting Company

"We are proud of you….[Even though] you are out of the country, still your energy and support is with us and with the suffered people of Afghanistan…."

~Director, Peace Education Organization

"I cannot find right words to express my gratitude to your extraordinary commitment, passion, patience and skills. I look forward to seeing you in near future either in the US or your second home, Afghanistan. Best regards,"

~University Professor

"This is the first time ever in the history of this country that the position of civil society is such focus on corruption related issues. There were numerous of conferences on Afghanistan in last one decade, but the issue of corruption was not a big topic and the position paper of the civil society for Tokyo is completely different from the previous one and it is talking about corruption as an issue. So it shows that we are in the right direction and doing a good job. Such a strategic action can reflect the tireless efforts of anti-corruption activists and Shafafiyat has played a key role by engaging and informing civil society about the issues. In such a great moment I would like to share my feeling through this email to our champions...and congratulate them for such an enormous outcome of their efforts.... In words it is so difficult to explain the feelings I have about you and your great contributions to my country. I am sure that every single one who has met you have the same impression."

~Chairman, Civil Society Organization

Appendix B:
Counterinsurgency Guidance and Notes

The following excerpts from U.S. counterinsurgency manuals and guidance show that most of the points I have made in the above text are supported in theory by military doctrine and instruction. Unfortunately we have not made an actual earnest attempt to put these ideas into practice.

"ISAF Commander's COIN Guidance: 24 Points,"
from a wall-poster at a Forward Operating Base
(FOB) in Eastern Afghanistan:

1. Secure and serve the population
2. Live among the people
3. Help confront the culture of impunity
4. Help Afghans build accountability government
5. Pursue the enemy relentlessly
6. Fight hard and fight with discipline
7. Identify corrupt officials
8. Hold what we secure
9. Foster lasting relationships
10. Money is ammo; don't put it in the wrong hands
11. Be a good guest
12. Consult and build relationships, but not just with those who seek us out
13. Walk
14. Act as one team
15. Partner with ANSF
16. Promote local re-integration
17. Be first with the truth
18. Fight the information war aggressively
19. Manage expectations

20. Live our values
21. Maintain continuity thru transactions
22. Empower subordinates
23. Win the battle of wits
24. Exercise initiative

Excerpts from COMISAF (Commander, ISAF) Counterinsurgency Guidance, 1 August, 2010—signed by General David Petraeus:

"Secure and serve the population. The decisive terrain is the human terrain. The people are the center of gravity. Only by providing them security and earning their trust and confidence can the Afghan government and ISAF prevail."

"Live among the people. We can't commute to the fight. Position joint bases and combat outposts as close to those we're seeking to secure as is feasible. Decide on locations with input from our partners and after consultation with local citizens and informed by intelligence and security assessments."

"Foster lasting solutions. Help our Afghan partners create good governance and enduring security. Avoid compromises with malign actors that achieve short-term gains at the expense of long-term stability. Think hard before pursuing initiatives that may not be sustainable in the long run. When it comes to projects, small is often beautiful."

"Be a good guest. Treat the Afghan people and their property with respect. Think about how we drive, how we patrol, how we relate to people, and how we help the community. View our actions through the eyes of the

Afghans and, together with our partners, consult with elders before pursuing new initiatives and operations."

"Consult and build relationships, but not just with those who seek us out. Earn the people's trust, talk to them, ask them questions, and learn about their lives. Inquire about social dynamics, frictions, local histories, and grievances. Hear what they say. Be aware of others in the room and how their presence may affect the answers you get. Cross-check information and make sure you have the full story. Avoid knee-jerk responses based on first impressions. Don't be a pawn in someone else's game. Spend time, listen, consult, and drink lots of tea."

"Walk. Stop by, don't drive by. Patrol on foot whenever possible and engage the population. Take off your sunglasses. Situational awareness can only be gained by interacting face-to-face, not separated by ballistic glass or Oakleys."

"Partner with ANSF. Live, eat, train, and operate together. Depend on one another. Hold each other accountable at all echelons down to trooper level. Help our ANSF partners achieve excellence. Respect them and listen to them. Be a good role model."

"Empower subordinates. Resource to enable decentralized action. Push assets and authorities down to those who most need them and can actually use them. Flatten reporting chains (while maintaining hierarchical decision chains). Remember that it is those at tactical levels—the so-called 'strategic sergeants' and 'strategic captains'—who turn big ideas in counterinsurgency operations into reality on the ground."

Excerpts from *Counterinsurgency Field Manual—Tactics, Intelligence, Host Nation Forces, Airpower* by Lt. General David Petraeus, 2008:

"Understand what motivates the people and how to mobilize them. Knowing why and how the insurgents are getting followers is essential. This requires knowing the real enemy, not a cardboard cutout. Insurgents are adaptive, resourceful, and probably from the area.... Much of their success may stem from bad government policies or security forces that alienate the local populace."

"Identify and Use Talent. Not everyone is good at counterinsurgency. Many leaders do not understand it, and some who do cannot execute it... people able to intuitively grasp, master, and execute COIN techniques are rare. Learn how to spot these people and put them into positions where they can make a difference. Rank may not indicate the required talent. In COIN operations, a few good Soldiers and Marines under a smart junior noncommissioned officer doing the right things can succeed, while a large force doing the wrong things will fail."

"Build Trusted Networks. Once the unit settles into the AO [Area of Operations], its next task is to build trusted networks. This is the true meaning of the phrase 'hearts and minds...'. Over time, successful trusted networks grow like roots into the populace. They displace enemy networks, which forces enemies into the open, letting military forces seize the initiative and destroy the insurgents. Trusted networks are diverse. They include local allies, community leaders, and local security forces. Networks should also include nongovernmental organizations (NGOs), other friendly or neutral nonstate actors...and the media."

"Building trusted networks begins with conducting village and neighborhood surveys to identify community needs. Then follow through to meet them, build common interests, and mobilize popular support. This is the true main effort; everything else is secondary. Actions that help build trusted networks support the COIN effort. Actions that undermine trust or disrupt these networks— even those that provide a short-term military advantage— help the enemy."

"COIN operations can be characterized as armed social work. It includes attempts to redress basic social and political problems while being shot at."

"Effective CMO [civil-military operations] require close cooperation with national, international, and local interagency partners. These partners are not under military control. Many NGOs, for example, do not want to be too closely associated with military forces because they need to preserve their perceived neutrality. Interagency cooperation may involve a shared analysis of the problem, building a consensus that allows synchronization of military and interagency efforts. The military's role is to provide protection, identify needs, facilitate CMO, and use improvements in social conditions as leverage to build networks and mobilize the populace."

Appendix C:
Glossary of (Mostly Military) Terms

ANA: Afghan National Army
ANP: Afghan National Police
ANSF: Afghan National Security Forces
AO: Area of Operations
APH or AfPak Hands: Afghanistan-Pakistan Hands
CAG: Commander's Action Group
CJIATF: Combined, Joint, Inter-Agency Task Force
CJCS: Chairman of the Joint Chiefs of Staff
CMO: Civil-military operations
COIN: Counterinsurgency
COMISAF: Commander, ISAF
CSTC-A: Combined Security Transition Command –
    Afghanistan
CVI: Civil Vision International
FATA: Federally Administered Tribal Areas in Pakistan
FET: Female Engagement Team
FOB: Forward Operating Base
FORTE: Family, Occupation, Recreation, Transportation,
    Education
IED: Improvised Explosive Device
ISAF: International Security Assistance Force
ISI: Pakistan's Directorate for Inter-Services Intelligence,
    or CIA equivalent
NGO: Non-Governmental Organization
NTM-A: NATO Training Mission – Afghanistan
PRT: Provincial Reconstruction Team
USA: U.S. Army
USAF: U.S. Air Force

Acknowledgments

This manuscript owes much to the encouragement and feedback of Colonel Ed Jakes (who first urged me to write an after-action report when I returned from deployment), Colonel Tim Kirk (whose inspiration is evident in both word and deed throughout the text), Dr. Davood Moradian, Rufus Phillips, Rob Grant, Dr. John Hervey, and Dr. Emily Hervey. I am so grateful for their many inputs and improvements to these pages.

Cover design by Tim Kirk.

Selected Bibliography

Ambinder, Marc and Goldberg, Jeffrey. "The Ally from Hell," *The Atlantic Magazine*, December 2011.
http://www.theatlantic.com/magazine/archive/2011/12/the-ally-from-hell/8730/

Alexander, Chris. *The Long Way Back: Afghanistan's Quest for Peace.* New York, NY: HarperCollins Publishers, 2011.

Bajoria, Jayshree. "The Taliban in Afghanistan." *The Council on Foreign Relations,* 2011.
http://www.cfr.org/afghanistan/taliban-afghanistan/p10551#p6

Brazinsky, Gregg. *Nation Building in South Korea.* Chapel Hill, NC: University of North Carolina Press, 2009.

Chandrasekaran, Rajiv. *Little America: The War Within the War for Afghanistan.* New York, NY: Knopf, Borzoi Books (Random House, Inc), 2012.

Coll, Steve. *Ghost Wars: The Secret History of the CIA, Afghanistan, and bin Laden, from the Soviet Invasion to September 10.* New York, NY: Penguin Books, 2004.

Dyer, Emily. "The 'War on Women' Being Waged in Afghanistan." *The Telegraph,* 26 June, 2012.
http://www.telegraph.co.uk/news/worldnews/asia/afghanistan/9356291/The-war-on-women-being-waged-in-Afghanistan.html

Fishtein, Paul and Wilder, Andrew. "Winning Hearts and Minds? Examining the Relationship between Aid and Security in Afghanistan." Feinstein International Center (Tufts University), 2011.
http://sites.tufts.edu/feinstein/files/2012/01/WinningHearts-Final.pdf

Galula, David. *The Pacification of Algeria, 1956-1958.* Santa Monica, CA: RAND Corporation, 2006.

Glavin, Terry. *Come from the Shadows: The Long and Lonely Struggle for Peace in Afghanistan.* Vancouver BC, Canada: Douglas & McIntyre, 2011.

Kirk, Timothy. "AfPak Hands: A Personal Account from the Field." Globe Magazine, September, 2010. http://www.scribd.com/doc/65426077/Globe-2010-Final

Kuehn, Felix and Strick van Linschoten, Alex. *Poetry of the Taliban.* New York: Columbia University Press, 2012.

Nagl, John A. "A 'Better War' in Afghanistan." Prepared Statement for Congressional Testimony, 16 September, 2009. http://www.cnas.org/files/documents/publications/CNASTestim ony_Nagl_SFRC_September_16_2009.pdf

Petraeus, David, Lt General. *Counterinsurgency Field Manual: Tactics, Intelligence, Host Forces, Airpower.* Department of the Army, 2008.

Reidel, Bruce. *Deadly Embrace: Pakistan, America, and the Future of Global Jihad.* Washington, DC: The Brookings Institution, 2011.

Tomsen, Peter. *The Wars of Afghanistan: Messianic Terrorism, Tribal Conflicts, and the Failures of Great Powers.* New York, NY: PublicAffairs (Perseus Books Group), 2011.

Senior officer debrief for Major General John H. Cushman, Combined Arms Research Library: http://cgsc.cdmhost.com/cdm/singleitem/collection/p4013coll11 /id/1481/rec/4

White Paper of the Interagency Policy Group's Report on U.S. Policy toward Afghanistan and Pakistan" http://www.whitehouse.gov/assets/documents/Afghanistan-Pakistan_White_Paper.pdf

Enjoy Afghanistan Handbook, Interlit Foundation (2004). http://www.interlitfoundation.org/ Afghan culture and language

resources by Interlit also at:
www.about-afghanistan.com/hospitality-afghanistan-culture.html

"Secret Pakistan," BBC documentary (2012).
http://www.youtube.com/watch?v=qSinK-dVrig

"Barack Obama on The War in Afghanistan," *The Political Guide* (4 March, 2011).
http://www.thepoliticalguide.com/Profiles/President/US/Barack_Obama/Views/The_War_in_Afghanistan/

"Strategic Glimpses" briefings developed by Colonel Tim Kirk, USAF.

Maps courtesy of OpenStreetMap© contributors at openstreetmap.org.

Endnotes

[1] See full senior officer debrief at
http://cgsc.cdmhost.com/cdm/singleitem/collection/p4013coll
11/id/1481/rec/4

[2] Read more in a brief article called "What Went Wrong in
Afghanistan?" by Seth Jones, author of *In the Graveyard of
Empires: America's War in Afghanistan:*
http://www.foreignpolicy.com/articles/2013/03/04/what_went_
wrong?page=0,3

[3] Carl von Clausewitz, *On War,* ed. and trans. Michael Howard
and Peter Paret (Princeton, NJ: Princeton University Press,
1976; reprint 1984), pp. 88-89.

[4] For more on Pakistan's colonialist plans and methods see
Steve Coll, *Ghost Wars* (2004) and *DW* article "Taliban are
Pakistani Military Without Uniform"
http://www.dw.de/dw/article/0,,15939683,00.html

[5] Marc Ambinder and Jeffrey Goldberg, "The Ally From Hell"
(2011)
http://www.theatlantic.com/magazine/archive/2011/12/the-ally-
from-hell/8730/

[6] For details see "Deadly Shelling by Pakistan Into Afghanistan
Is Stoking Tensions"
http://www.nytimes.com/2011/07/04/world/asia/04afghanistan.h
tml and "Pakistan Was Consulted Before Fatal Hit, U.S. Says"
for more detailed accounts:
http://online.wsj.com/article/SB10001424052970203833104577
072771910500442.html?mod=googlenews_wsj

[7] Alex Strick van Linschoten and Felix Kuehn, *Poetry of the
Taliban* (Columbia University Press, 2012), page 29.

[8] See Chris Alexander's account in *The Long Way Back* (2011),
pp. 128-129 and Steve Coll's *Ghost Wars* (2004) for a detailed
account of Pakistan's strategy in Afghanistan. Points that follow
in this section are drawn from these books and the insights of
other scholars in Afghanistan.

[9] As described in communications with Dr. Davood Moradian,
President of Afghanistan Institute for Strategic Studies and
former senior advisor at Afghan Ministry of Foreign Affairs

[10] This public domain map depicts the region with the Durand Line as the modern border between Afghanistan and Pakistan, along with the shaded area roughly depicting the historic Pashtunistan and Baluchistan ethnic areas.

[11] For further details on Pakistan's fear of dismemberment see Nitin Pai, "Why Pakistan Interferes in Afghanistan," http://acorn.nationalinterest.in/2012/05/25/why-pakistan-interferes-in-afghanistan/

[12] Barnett R Rubin, a fellow at the Council on Foreign Relations, testified on the situation in Afghanistan before the United States Senate Committee on Foreign Relations in 1999. See an excerpt from his presentation at: http://in.rediff.com/news/1999/dec/30us1.htm

[13] "It is noted that the 'basic preconditions' for the overthrow of [Mohammed] Daoud in April 1978 'flowed from the objective domestic political and economic development of the country after 1973.' Daoud expressed the interests and class position of bourgeois landowners and rightist nationalist forces, and therefore was not capable of carrying out a reformation 'in the interests of the broad laboring masses,' primarily agricultural reform.... This led to an 'abrupt sharpening of the contradictions between the Daoud regime and its class supporters and the fundamental interests of the working masses, the voice of which is the PDPA.'" from "Political Letter from USSR Ambassador to Afghanistan A. Puzanov to Soviet Foreign Ministry, 'About the Domestic Political Situation in the DRA,' (notes)" May 31, 1978, History and Public Policy Program Digital Archive, Based on notes taken by Odd Arne Westad on materials at the Center for the Storage of Contemporary Documentation (TsKhSD), fond (f.) 5, opis (op.) 75, delo (d.) 1179, listy (ll.) 2-17 http://www.digitalarchive.org/document/113255

[14] The Woodrow Wilson International Center for Scholars has an excellent history archive of translated Soviet reports on pre-invasion atmospherics in Afghanistan at http://www.digitalarchive.org/collection/76/soviet-invasion-of-afghanistan

[15] As described by the Center for Islamic Pluralism, "the Inter-Service Intelligence...sowed the dragon seeds to sprout as the legions of jihadis (holy warriors) joined in a common

cause to make war against the enemies of Islam preached by Taliban's chieftain Mullah Omar and al Qaida's Osama bin Laden." at http://www.islamicpluralism.org/296/pakistans-crisis-global-concern

[16] This is a very conservative estimate, since many sources cite numbers upwards of 30,000. In a 1999 letter to the people of America, Ahmad Shah Massoud wrote, "Aside from receiving military logistics, fuel and arms from Pakistan, our intelligence reports indicate that more than 28,000 Pakistani citizens, including paramilitary personnel and military advisers are part of the Taliban occupation forces in various parts of Afghanistan." See http://www.afghan-web.com/documents/let-masood.html

[17] See, for example: "Taliban's Whipping of Ghor Couple Reminds of Atrocities," http://centralasiaonline.com/en_GB/articles/caii/features/pakista n/main/2013/03/04/feature-01 and a brief historical account of "The Taliban in Afghanistan" by Jayshree Bajoria, http://www.cfr.org/afghanistan/taliban-afghanistan/p10551#p6

[18] Nitin Pai is Co-Founder & Fellow for Geopolitics at The Takshashila Institution. See his article, "Why Pakistan Interferes in Afghanistan," http://acorn.nationalinterest.in/2012/05/25/why-pakistan-interferes-in-afghanistan/

[19] See Bruce Riedel's *Deadly Embrace: Pakistan, America, and the Future of Global Jihad* (2011) for incisive analysis on the nature of the problem. Also see BBC documentary "Secret Pakistan," http://www.youtube.com/watch?v=qSinK-dVrig

[20] http://www.fas.org/sgp/crs/row/R41856.pdf, and from Newsweek magazine: "Officials at the U.S. Embassy in Islamabad have alleged that Pakistan misspent some 70 percent of the U.S. funds that paid the Pakistani military..." at http://www.thedailybeast.com/newsweek/2009/10/21/about-those-billions.html

[21] As quoted in CNN's Security Blog at http://security.blogs.cnn.com/2012/01/24/violence-spikes-in-key-afghan-regions/

[22] List from "Strategic Glimpses" briefing developed by Colonel Tim Kirk, USAF, used by permission

[23] "White Paper of the Interagency Policy Group's Report on U.S. Policy toward Afghanistan and Pakistan" http://www.whitehouse.gov/assets/documents/Afghanistan-Pakistan_White_Paper.pdf

[24] John Nagl, "A 'Better War' in Afghanistan," Congressional Testimony (2009), http://www.cnas.org/files/documents/publications/CNASTestim ony_Nagl_SFRC_September_16_2009.pdf

[25] Many sources reflect these views; for an example of the impact on women see Emily Dyer's article, "The 'War on Women' Being Waged in Afghanistan," http://www.telegraph.co.uk/news/worldnews/asia/afghanist an/9356291/The-war-on-women-being-waged-in-Afghanistan.html

[26] Many recent reports cite increasing ANSF capabilities, such as this one in the Eurasia Review (June 12, 2013) http://www.eurasiareview.com/12062013-isaf-says-response-to-taliban-attacks-shows-ansf-ready-to-assume-leading-role/ Many others, like a 2012 editorial in *The Daily Outlook Afghanistan* cite the mounting cost, with ANSF casualties increasing as NATO casualties decrease. In http://outlookafghanistan.net/editorialdetail.php?post_id=5844

[27] Paul Fishtein and Andrew Wilder, "Winning Hearts and Minds? Examining the Relationship between Aid and Security in Afghanistan." Feinstein International Center (Tufts University), 2011. http://sites.tufts.edu/feinstein/files/2012/01/WinningHearts-Final.pdf

[28] Ibid.

[29] David Galula, *The Pacification of Algeria 1956-1958* (2006), pp. 246-247.

[30] Also see Lt. General David Petraeus, *Counterinsurgency Field Manual: Tactics, Intelligence, Host Forces, Airpower* (Department of the Army, 2008).

[31] See speech at Woodrow Wilson International Center and interview from trip to Afghanistan: http://www.thepoliticalguide.com/Profiles/President/US/Barack _Obama/Views/The_War_in_Afghanistan/

[32] Terry Glavin, *Come from the Shadows: The Long and Lonely Struggle for Peace in Afghanistan,* 2011, p. 29.

[33] This problem of short-termism and its impact on counterinsurgency success is outlined in the U.S. Army's *Counterinsurgency Field Manual: Tactics, Intelligence, Host Forces, Airpower* by then Lt. General David Petraeus (2008).

[34] For specifics, see Appendix C: Counterinsurgency Guidance and Notes

[35] See Appendix C for excerpts

[36] This report has not focused on describing the results of our work, but rather the methods, approaches, and best practices that I believe made them possible. Appendix A includes perspectives of Afghans on the value of our efforts.

[37] CJCS Instruction 1630.01, 3 September 2010, http://www.jcs.mil/page.aspx?id=52

[38] Ibid.

[39] Written by Eugene Burdick and William J. Lederer, *The Ugly American* was first published in 1958 and is a must-read for anyone thinking about American engagement abroad.

[40] © Tim Kirk, used by permission

[41] *Enjoy Afghanistan* Handbook, Interlit Foundation www.about-afghanistan.com/hospitality-afghanistan-culture.html

[42] See http://www.afghan-web.com/documents/let-masood.html

[43] Rufus Phillips, *Why Vietnam Matters: An Eyewitness Account of Lessons Not Learned* (Annapolis, Maryland: Naval Institute Press, 2008), 305-306.

[44] In a 1998 letter to the American people, Ahmad Shah Massoud wrote: "We consider this as part of our duty to defend humanity against the scourge of intolerance, violence and fanaticism. But the international community and the democracies of the world should not waste any valuable time, and instead play their critical role to assist in any way possible the valiant people of Afghanistan overcome the obstacles that exist on the path to freedom, peace, stability and prosperity." Read the entire letter at: http://www.afghan-web.com/documents/let-masood.html

[45] Rufus Phillips, *Why Vietnam Matters: An Eyewitness Account of Lessons Not Learned* (Annapolis, Maryland: Naval Institute Press, 2008), pages 305-306.

[46] As calculated by Richard Miller in *Funding Extended Conflicts: Korea, Vietnam, and the War on Terror* (Prager, 2007), page 39.